Kunda Eats

Best New Restaurants in America
2012 Edition

M.V. KUNDA
ED IM

KundaEats.com

Vayu Publishing
New York

For our dads, Dr. Gopal Das Kunda and Mr. Kil Chang Im, who inspired us through their tireless work ethic, taught us through their moral values, and motivated us through their constant encouragement.

Table of Contents

Introduction

Kunda Eats

Best New Restaurants in America
2012 Edition

Introduction

Welcome to the 2012 Edition of Kunda Eats Best New Restaurants in America, the most comprehensive and informative compilation of such information to be found anywhere.

With over 200 entries, representing 35 states and 53 cities, our list encompasses all types and manner of dining establishments, from high-end "gastro temples" to "cheap eats." Using our own unique methodology, our egalitarian approach does not discriminate based on size, cost, décor, location, or type of cuisine. Our primary mission is to provide you with the most complete list of the best new restaurants in the United States, period.

We believe that a great dining experience, in which the food, service, and atmosphere combine to create a memorable moment, can be had just as easily at a small food truck as it can at a fancy, white-tablecloth restaurant. Our approach gives as much attention and praise to a great restaurant in a small farm town as it does to one in a big cosmopolitan city. In fact, we may give the former even more attention, aware of the uphill battle it faces for recognition from traditional food media outlets.

This past year saw a variety of interesting restaurants open throughout the country. There is no question that it has been an exciting and transformative year in the culinary world, and the landscape is quickly evolving. Talented chefs are no longer content to simply re-create mundane menus based on classic restaurant fare, but are instead being bold and aggressive. Chefs are now respecting the diner's intelligence and willingness to try something new, unique, and interesting. Nowhere is this more apparent than in Asian cuisine, where chefs appreciate the fact that Americans have been hungering for authentic Indian, Vietnamese, Thai, and Chinese cuisine, instead of the typical watered down versions.

Increasingly, chefs understand that if the food is fresh, interesting, and prepared with quality ingredients, the diner will respect and appreciate being taken on a wonderful gastronomic journey.

While conducting research for the book, we happened to notice several culinary trends that were prevalent, providing a barometer that lets us know what direction chefs and restaurants are gravitating toward.

Locally Sourced and Farm-to-Table

From small towns to big cities, many chefs are embracing this "local" philosophy. As an example, one restaurant in San Antonio only uses ingredients that can be sourced from within 150 miles, and they use no electricity in the kitchen. This ensures that all ingredients are fresh on a daily basis. Sourcing ingredients locally helps ensure that the food is fresh, while also helping the local purveyors and economy. Many diners are only too happy to support their local farms and dairies through restaurant proxy.

Gastropubs

We were surprised by how many Gastropubs were being opened throughout the country. While we would expect this in the larger cities, smaller cities and towns also embraced this trend. It serves to prove that upscale cuisine at affordable prices, coupled with large selections of craft beers, is a popular combination anywhere.

Global Influences

We keep hearing that the world is getting smaller, and this is evident even in the culinary scene. Chefs are more willing to challenge the palate by combining different influences from various cultures. American, Asian, European, Mediterranean, and South American cuisines, among others, are all seamlessly blended to create unique interpretations of classic cuisine. For example, one restaurant might offer a Korean influence mixed with southern soul food, while another might offer French cuisine combined with Indian or South American influences. This creates an exciting environment for diners as they now are able to taste bold new flavors infused in traditional dishes.

Innovation at Casual Restaurants

With the world in financial straits, some of the most innovative, unique, and interesting food is being prepared at small, casual restaurants and food trucks. Many of these restaurants are very limited in their size, with some only having 10 or 15 seats.

No longer is great food the exclusive domain of big expensive restaurants in the high rent districts of large cities. Today, talented chefs with limited budgets are going to small towns and opening modest restaurants with bold menus as exciting as those in the biggest cities in the world - and they are thriving. With the popularity of Facebook, Twitter, and other social networking media, it's possible for a chef in a non-traditional setting to gain a quick following. And, of course, Kunda Eats hopes to do its part every year by bringing attention to these chefs who are deserving of it.

Authentic Asian Restaurants

Of all the trends that we noticed, none surprised us more than seeing how many wonderful new authentic Asian restaurants opened in small towns throughout the country. One might expect this in the ethnic enclaves of New York, Los Angeles, or San Francisco, but it was surprising to see it occurring so successfully in Middle America.

This is not the usual watered down, "Americanized" Asian cuisine, but rather, authentic cuisine with recipes brought back from the homelands in India, Korea, Vietnam, Thailand, China, etc. It is unique, bold, flavorful, spicy, and exciting, and diners everywhere are embracing it. As two Asians (an Indian and a Korean) who founded Kunda Eats, this is a trend that we hope continues to flourish in cities and small towns throughout the country.

We hope you find this compilation of Best New Restaurants helpful, fun, and educational. If this book encourages you try even one new restaurant that gives you a memorable dining experience, then we feel we've done our job.

We also welcome you to visit our website at www.kundaeats.com, where you will find even more information to help find the best dining experiences in over 200 cities around the world. Presented in a simple format, the comprehensive information has been compiled from a variety of sources, including local media, food blogs, major publications, crowd sourced sites, and food critics.

Be sure to also visit our Review Table, in which we compile the latest restaurant reviews for New York, Chicago, and San Francisco.

Our mission at Kunda Eats is to provide you with the most comprehensive "one stop" resource for researching and finding the best dining experiences in major cities around the world. We've done all of the research, so you don't have to.

Kunda Eats.....always your local compass.

Heirloom Market BBQ

BBQ   www.heirloommarketbbq.com
2243 Akers Mill Road, Suite 110
Atlanta, GA 30339
770.612.2502

- Chef Jiyeon Lee (Repast), a former pop music star in her native homeland of Korea, and chef Cody Taylor (Ritz-Carlton Buckhead, Repast), raised in Tennessee, respect the classic methods of BBQ while adding their own personal touches.
- Eschewing a single "type" of BBQ flavor, the chefs instead keep an open mind and borrow from all different types and styles of BBQ to create their own unique vision.
- Heirloom Market sources its pork and beef from a local family farm for items like brisket, pulled pork, burgers, and ribs.

Local Three Kitchen & Bar

Southern Farm-to-Table   www.localthree.com
3290 Northside Parkway
Atlanta, GA 30327
404.968.2700

- Employing a "Foie Gras in Flip Flops" approach, chef-owners Chris Hall (Canoe) and Todd Mussman (Muss & Turner's) have created a casual neighborhood joint with high quality food to match.
- Local Three's mantra is "you can't argue with delicious," and by focusing on food that is fresh, seasonal, sustainable, and local, they are clearly fulfilling their mission.
- Hall crafts a menu with dishes like chicken pot pie, Georgia mountain trout, crispy duck leg cassoulet, and the famous McDowell burger (think "Coming to America").

One Eared Stag

Southern Fusion-Global   www.oneearedstag.com
1029 Edgewood Avenue   @oneearedstag
Atlanta, GA 30307
404.525.4479

- Originality, creativity, and a willingness to push the envelope appear to be chef Robert Phalen's (Mumbo Jumbo, Shaun's, Holy Taco) hallmarks at his new, innovative restaurant in Inman Park.
- Changing his menu often, Phalen is not afraid to take chances by utilizing numerous influences from various cultures around the globe.
- Adventurous food lovers will feel at home here, with dishes like rabbit loin, fried chicken necks with kimchi, roasted beef tongue, and skate wing, but there's plenty for conservative eaters as well.

Viande Rouge

American-French Steakhouse   www.vrsteakhouse.com
9810 Medlock Bridge Road   @ViandeRouge
Johns Creek, GA 30097
770.623.4959

- With the perfect name for a steakhouse, chef-owner Marc Sublette (Trattoria One 41) injects a heavy French influence into a quintessentially American cuisine.
- Normal steakhouse mainstays, such as New York strip and Delmonico rib eye, are joined by decidedly French fare like duck à l'orange and boeuf bourguignon.
- Be sure to save room for the bananas Foster flambéed with bourbon and Schnapps, or the chocolate soufflé.

For a complete list of Atlanta food resources, visit kundaeats.com/atlanta.

Barley Swine

Pork and Beer   www.barleyswine.com
2024 South Lamar Boulevard   @BarleySwine
Austin, TX 78704
512.394.8150

- Barley Swine is food trailer legend Bryce Gilmore's (Food & Wine's Best New Chefs 2011) first foray into the brick and mortar world.
- Though the locally-sourced, small plates menu changes with the seasons, the constants of pork and beer (and egg) remain steadfast. For dessert, think foie gras funnel cake.
- Just up the road from Gilmore's iconic Odd Duck Farm-to-Trailer, the restaurant utilizes communal tables in a small, lively space… with a roof.

Congress

Natural American   www.congressaustin.com
200 Congress Avenue   @CongressAustin
Austin, TX 78701
512.827.2755

- Every night, chef David Bull (Driskill Grill) and chef de cuisine Rebecca Meeker customize a new prix fixe three and seven-course fine dining menu based on available seasonal ingredients.
- Bull describes this culinary approach as "Natural American."
- The white-tablecloth restaurant itself is part of a triumvirate concept alongside a casual bistro (Second Bar + Kitchen) and bar (Bar Congress) located within the downtown Austonian condominium complex.

Uchiko

Japanese/SE Asian Seafood   www.uchiaustin.com
4200 North Lamar Boulevard #140   @UchikoAustin
Austin, TX 78756
512.916.4808

- Fresh off winning the 2011 Best Southwest Chef at the James Beard Awards, Tyson Cole opens his second restaurant aptly translated "child of Uchi (his first restaurant)."
- The menu draws inspiration from Japanese coastal farm culture with a twist of Southeast Asia thanks to executive chef Paul Qui (Top Chef season 9 winner). Brag dishes include White Bass Sakama Mushi and Squid Ika Yaki.
- The North Austin restaurant prides itself in using sustainable fish suppliers and surprising diners with situational "bonus" dishes or bites.

For a complete list of Austin food resources, visit kundaeats.com/austin.

Corner BYOB

Continental-Comfort Food   www.cornerbyob.com
850 West 36th Street
Baltimore, MD 21211
443.869.5075

- Corner BYOB is chef Bernard Dehaene's (Mannequin Pis) latest venture and his focus this time is to create "refined peasant fare" aka comfort food with a rustic approach.
- Dehaene's cuisine can best be described as continental with New American ingredients and overtones of European and Belgian influence.
- Roasted bone marrow, Resurrection Ale beef stew, and mussels by the kilopot are a few of the signature dishes.

Demi

New American   www.demirestaurant.com
510 East Belvedere Avenue   @DemiBaltimore
Baltimore, MD 21212
443.278.9001

- Demi is a new restaurant collaboration from owner Dan Chaustit (Crush) and executive chef Tae Strain (Public).
- Located in the lower level of Chaustit's established restaurant Crush, Demi forges its own unique identity thanks to Strain's globally infused interpretations of traditional American fare.
- Working with the help of only a single cook, Strain somehow manages to create a series of artfully presented small plate dishes, each with a unique flavor that belies its small size.
- Try to sit at one of the 8 stools overlooking the open kitchen so you can watch Strain prepare specialties like the six-minute egg, maple- pork belly, and crab-crusted salmon.

Meet 27

American-South Asian Bistro   www.meet27.com
127 West 27th Street   @meet27now
Baltimore, MD 21218
410.585.8121

- Complementing his Indian upbringing, chef Richard D'Souza (Sweet Sin Bakery) brings a wide range of flavors from all over the globe in his unique American Bistro.
- D'Souza's menu explodes with a fusion of South Asian and Caribbean flavors, offering a selection of local, all-natural, organic, and homemade foods.
- Meet 27 offers something special for everyone, whether it's carnivorous, gluten free, vegan, vegetarian, or soy free.
- Global influences are readily seen in items such as vindaloo pork, vada pao burger, chili paneer, and the veggie platter.

Thames Street Oyster House

Seafood   www.thamesstreetoysterhouse.com
1728 Thames Street   @TSOH2011
Baltimore, MD 21231
443.449.7726

- Owner Candace Beattie brings a New England style seafood bistro to Baltimore, offering traditional Maryland, Mid-Atlantic and New England seafood dishes.
- All of the seafood is delivered fresh daily, never frozen, and ingredients are sourced locally and sustainably whenever possible from the Atlantic waters.
- Chef Eric Houseknecht's menu offers traditional seafood dishes such as cast iron crab cake, bouillabaisse, shrimp ceviche, New England lobster rolls, and grilled octopus.

For a complete list of Baltimore food resources, visit kundaeats.com/baltimore.

Ollie Irene

Gastropub   www.ollieirene.com
2713 Culver Road
Birmingham, AL 35223
205.769.6034

- Naming the restaurant after his grandmother, Chef Chris Newsome (Bottega Café, Highlands Bar and Grill) brings the gastropub concept to Birmingham, offering haute cuisine in a casual environment.
- Newsome focuses on using fresh ingredients sourced locally, regionally, and seasonally and changes the menu accordingly.
- Fresh, local ingredients are evident when you try dishes like boudin balls, slow-cooked pork shoulder, chicken liver terrine, or the popular ham plate.
- Sit at the bar, which is made from a 140 year old slab of oak, and let bartender Zak Kittle make you a handcrafted drink.

For a complete list of Birmingham food resources, visit kundaeats.com/birmingham.

7

5 Corners Kitchen

New American-French   www.5cornerskitchen.com
2 School Street
Marblehead, MA 01945
781.631.5550

- Chef Barry Edelman (Aquitaine, Lumiere) returned to his hometown of Marblehead with this New American-French bistro.
- After a gangbusters start filled with accolades and lines, 5 Corners Kitchen was beset with a devastating two-alarm fire that destroyed everything.
- With help from the community, the completely re-built and expanded restaurant plans to reopen in the summer of 2012.

Bondir

New American   www.bondircambridge.com
279A Broadway   @jwadebond
Cambridge, MA 02139
617.661.0009

- Chef Jason Bond (Beacon Hill Bistro) practices a kind of "root-cellar" cuisine which depends heavily on a network of New England food purveyors and producers. Having grown up in a Wyoming farm, he is particularly fond of heritage vegetables and rare livestock breeds.
- Bondir's menu changes daily (with recurring standards) based on available ingredients. The constant menu refreshes can be tracked online at bondircambridge.com.
- The small, cozy Cambridge space seats 28 and features a centerpiece fireplace.

Island Creek Oyster Bar

Seafood-Oyster Bar   www.islandcreekoysterbar.com
500 Commonwealth Avenue   @ICOBar
Boston, MA 02215
617.532.5300

- Grower-turned-restaurateur Skip Bennett brings his coveted bivalves farm-direct to Fenway Park's Hotel Commonwealth.
- Chef Jeremy Sewall's (Lineage) menu is heavy on sustainable "New England shore food." The popular Mrs. Bennett's Seafood Casserole can be ordered family style.
- Island Creek Oysters' beds supply the best chefs in the country including Thomas Keller.

Legal Harborside (Floor 2)

Seafood   www.legalseafoods.com
270 Northern Avenue   @legalseafoods
Boston, MA 02210
617.477.2900

- The 20,000 square foot crown jewel of the Legal Seafood empire spans three floors making it the largest restaurant in Boston. The first floor showcases the traditional menu with a bonus oyster bar and fish market. The third floor boasts a retractable roof sky lounge.
- … But it's the second floor that lands them on the Kunda Eats list. Here, Legal leverages its purchasing muscle with fish suppliers offering creative takes using premium ingredients (think caviar and hiramasa). The six course chef's tasting is one of the best bang for the buck deals in Boston.
- The waterfront Liberty Wharf location allows boaters to park their vessels to the restaurant's own slip pier.

Menton

French   www.mentonboston.com
354 Congress Street
Boston, MA 02210
617.737.0099

- After racking up numerous industry awards, Menton became the first Boston restaurant to receive the prestigious Relais & Chateaux designation.
- The French fine dining menu is seasonal and structured binarily: four courses prix fixe or chef's tasting.
- The floor price is around $100 per person, and with add-on options like Ostera caviar and "Château" wines, bring plastic.
- This restaurant is the third in owner Barbara Lynch's Fort Point trilogy (Drink, Sportello).

Trade

New American   www.trade-boston.com
540 Atlantic Avenue   @tradeboston
Boston, MA 02210
617.451.1234

- Cambridge veteran and Beard winner Jody Adams (Top Chef Masters) crosses the Charles River to collaborate with Rialto chums Sean Griffing and Eric Papachristos.
- Trade, located in the Atlantic Wharf, sources local ingredients to create dishes with heavy international influences.
- Flatbreads are a particular specialty of the house with interesting topping combinations like salt cod, and lamb sausage with eggplant (just don't ask for frozen goat leg).

For a complete list of Boston food resources, visit kundaeats.com/boston.

Blue Monk

Belgian Gastropub   www.bluemonkbflo.com
727 Elmwood Avenue   @BlueMonkBflo
Buffalo, NY 14222
716.882.6665

- Whether it's named after the blue-robed Belgian monks who have brewed some of the world's finest beer for centuries, or for jazz pianist Thelonius Monk, one thing we know is that Blue Monk is the first gastropub in Buffalo.
- With a Belgian-focused menu of traditional European pub fare, you'll find offerings such as Belgian onion soup, braised short rib sandwich, and duck confit reuben.
- Complementing the menu is a large selection of Belgian and American craft brews, including 32 on tap alone.

Lloyd's Taco Truck

Mexican American Food Truck   www.whereslloyd.com
Buffalo, NY   @whereslloyd
Variable Locations (check Twitter)
716.863.978

- The idea for Lloyd's Taco Truck was born when childhood friends Peter Cimino and Chris Dorsaneo realized there were no affordable, quality street food options in Buffalo.
- Delivering high-end food and service at street level prices, Lloyd's is a traveling Buffalo food experience that serves up fun, fresh, Mexican-American tacos.
- Follow the truck's location on Twitter so you can try menu staples like tomatillo pork tacos, braised beef burritos, and tricked out nachos.

For a complete list of Buffalo food resources, visit kundaeats.com/buffalo.

Pistou

Contemporary American
61 Main Street
Burlington, VT 05401
802.540.1783

www.pistou-vt.com
@PistouVT

- Chef-co-owner Max Mackinnon may only be 25 years old, but this graduate of the French Culinary Institute in New York City has a knowledge of gastronomy that is well beyond his age.
- Pistou features contemporary American cuisine prepared with both classic and modern French technique while using fresh, local, seasonal ingredients of the highest quality.
- Mackinnon has developed relationships with local farmers, butchers, and purveyors, gaining access to the freshest, high quality ingredients in order to create his ever changing menu.
- Among the dishes you might find are veal cheek and sweetbreads, pork belly and chicken thigh, and day boat scallops.

Husk

Southern   www.huskrestaurant.com
76 Queen Street   @HuskRestaurant
Charleston, SC 29401
843.577.2500

- James Beard Award-winning Chef Sean Brock (Lemaire, McCrady's) set out to prove that Southern food belongs among the best, and he did just that with his new restaurant.
- Brock creates his menu throughout the day, responding to the fresh ingredients his local purveyors are able to supply at the moment.
- "If it doesn't come from the South, it's not coming through the door," states Brock, and you'll thank him when you taste creations like deviled eggs with pickled okra and trout roe, stuffed quail, and country fried lamb.

The Macintosh

New American   www.themacintoshcharleston.com
479 King Street
Charleston, SC 29403
843.789.4299

- Chef Jeremiah Bacon (Le Bernardin, Per Se, Carolina's) embraces a local-first philosophy and uses his long standing relationships with farmers and purveyors to create an original menu that focuses on classic and seasonal favorites.
- The menu is a celebration of the quality of Charleston's local produce, meats, and seafood, and offers such signature dishes as grilled deckle, braised rabbit, hot and sour pork belly soup, and local grilled triggerfish.

Two Boroughs Larder

Seasonal American   www.twoboroughslarder.com
186 Coming Street   @2boroughslarder
Charleston, SC 29403
843.637.3722

- Two Boroughs Larder is a restaurant-market hybrid located in the Cannonborough-Elliotborough neighborhood.
- The husband and wife team of Josh and Heather Keeler run the kitchen with an emphasis on seasonal American ingredients (milk braised Alabama goat, crispy pig head, whole roasted lamb neck). High-end breakfast sandwiches using local egg and bacon are delightfully served all day.
- The "larder" half of the business features gourmet groceries and provisions. Popular items include hand poured soy wax candles, farm eggs, and South Carolina honey.
- Don't be surprised to see other chefs eating here.

For a complete list of Charleston food resources, visit kundaeats.com/charleston.

14

Bistro La Bon

Mediterranean   www.bistrolabon.com
1322 Central Avenue   @BistroLaBon
Charlotte, NC 28205
704.333.4646

- While the restaurant's name may sound like a French bistro, chef-owner Majid Amoorpour (Charlie Trotter's, Noble's) instead puts his focus on Mediterranean small plate dishes to illustrate gastronomic creativity.
- Amoorpour's team makes as many things from scratch as possible, including their breads, pastries and gnocchi, and the menu changes seasonally to take advantage of the freshest ingredients.
- Swedish meatballs, free range chicken, and Scottish salmon are just a few of the items that will grab your attention.

The Cowfish Sushi Burger Bar

Sushi-Burgers   www.thecowfish.com
4310 Sharon Road, Suite X05   @thecowfishSBB
Charlotte, NC 28211
704.365.1922

- Proclaiming itself the first and only "Sushi Burger Bar," the Cowfish is a one-of-a-kind dining experience, thriving on its ability to fuse two niche products seamlessly on the same menu thanks to executive chef David Lucarelli.
- Born of a desire to create a fun-loving environment that anyone can enjoy, the Cowfish focuses on offering both the best sushi and the best burger in town.
- Try the famous "Burgushi," which are unique sushi rolls created using burger components.

Midwood Smokehouse

BBQ   www.midwoodsmokehouse.com
1401 Central Avenue, Suite 101   @MidwoodBBQ
Charlotte, NC 28205
704.295.4227

- Noted Charlotte restaurateur, Frank Scibelli, (Big Daddy's Burger Bar, Paco's Tacos and Tequila), traveled throughout North Carolina, South Carolina, Texas, Kansas City, Memphis and other cities to learn from pit masters and gain inspiration for Midwood Smokehouse's menu.
- The smoker is a custom built, wood burning model and does not utilize natural gas or electricity to generate heat or smoke.
- You'll appreciate Scibelli's devotion and research when you try signature items like Carolina pork, Saint Louis style pork ribs, smoked sausage plate, and beef brisket.

For a complete list of Charlotte food resources, visit kundaeats.com/charlotte.

16

Peter Chang's China Grill

Chinese-Sichuan   www.peterchangscharlottesville.com
2162 Barracks Road
Charlottesville, VA 22903
434.244.9818

- Mythologized by the New Yorker's Calvin Trillin, the "disappearing chef" re-emerged in 2011, opening Peter Chang's China Grill.
- Once the personal chef to Chinese President Hu Jintao, Chang brings authentic mouth-numbing Sichuan cuisine to the foothills of the Blue Ridge Mountains.
- Recommendations? Start with plenty of ice water. Signature dishes include Dan Dan noodles, hot and numbing beef, dry fried eggplant, and anything with duck.

For a complete list of Charlottesville food resources, visit kundaeats.com/charlottesville.

17

Arami

Japanese-Sushi   www.aramichicago.com
1829 West Chicago Avenue   @AramiChicago
Chicago, IL 60622
312. 243.1535

- Chef B.K. Park (Mirai, Aria, Meiji) tends to the basics of Japanese cuisine using fresh, high quality ingredients.
- Sushi is the chef's specialty and he does not disappoint, showcasing his raw fish delicacies, such as whole aji and Geunkang nigiri, in artful presentations.
- If sushi doesn't appeal to your palate, try the Arami Ramen with pork belly, the broiled fish collar, or the togarashi seared tuna, which according to one critic is the one thing to try on the menu.

Autre Monde Cafe

Mediterranean   www.autremondecafe.com
6727 West Roosevelt Road   @AutreMondeCafe
Berwyn, IL 60402
708. 775.8122

- Autre Monde means "other world" in French, but chefs Beth Partridge and Dan Pancake's (Spiaggia, Mantuano Mediterranean Table) cuisine encompasses the entire Mediterranean region.
- With dishes like flatbreads, grilled octopus, butternut squash gnocchi, and guinea-hen sausage with oil-cured olives, the chefs focus on classic fare, done well, with fresh ingredients.
- The décor follows the Mediterranean theme and is bright and open, featuring an outdoor patio for alfresco dining in warmer weather.

Bistronomic

Modern Bistro   bistronomic.net
840 North Wabash Avenue   @bistronomicfood
Chicago, IL 60611
312.944.8400

- Chef Martial Noguier, formerly of Cafe des Architectes, and one sixtyblue, offers his modern take on the classic bistro.
- Bistronomic is combination of the terms "bistro" and "gastronomic," which summarizes Chef Noguier's goal of providing quality cuisine with a bistro's economic sensibilities.
- Interesting selections, such as oxtail ravioli, Amish chicken breast, cauliflower veloute with Pleasant Ridge cheese, and the chef's trademark dish, whole organic chicken, seem to support the chef's primary goals.

Chicago Cut Steakhouse

Steakhouse   www.chicagocutsteakhouse.com
300 North Lasalle Street   @ChicagoCut
Chicago, IL 60654
312.329.1800

- Chicago Cut is the latest venture from steakhouse veterans David Flom (Rosebud Steakhouse) and Matthew Moore (Smith & Wollensky).
- The steaks are dry aged in the restaurant for 30-45 days, which contributes to their excellent flavor and quality.
- Be sure to try the creamed spinach, which might just be the best in the city according to one critic.
- The restaurant has been garnering attention for presenting their wine list on iPads, so Luddites beware!

Davanti Enoteca

Italian   www.davantichicago.com
1359 West Taylor Street   @davanti_enoteca
Chicago, IL 60607
312. 226.5550

- Davanti Enoteca's lineage to the Purple Pig is evident in its DNA, as restaurateur Scott Harris (Purple Pig) and executive chef Jonathan Beatty (Purple Pig) team up again to bring rustic Italian food to Taylor Street.
- Once again using the small shared plate philosophy, Beatty's menu includes dishes such as linguine with shredded crabmeat and sea urchin, mascarpone polenta and ragu of the day, and uovo in raviolo 'San Domenico.'
- Prices are reasonable, with most dishes under $14.

Girl & The Goat

New American   www.girlandthegoat.com
809 West Randolph Street   @StephAndTheGoat
Chicago, IL 60607
312.492.6262

- Chef Stephanie Izard was the winner of Top Chef: Season Four, the only woman to ever win the title. Her previous restaurant, Scylla, was named one of Bon Appetit's 10 Best Restaurants in the Country.
- The menu is broken up into three categories: Meat, Vegetable, and Fish, while fresh bread is baked daily in house.
- The chef supports local farms in the area and tries to have fun with the menu, which includes dishes such as Escargot and Goat Balls, Crispy Pig Face, and Smokey Whipped Fat Back.
- The décor is casual and open with communal wood tables.

GT Fish & Oyster

Seafood-Oyster Bar   www.gtoyster.com
531 North Wells Street   @giuseppetentori
Chicago, IL 60654
312.929.3501

- Michelin Starred Chef Giuseppe Tentori (Charlie Trotter's, Boka Restaurant) brings his experiences growing up on a farm in Italy to the world of seafood by using locally sourced and seasonal ingredients.
- The chef utilizes the small, shared plate philosophy which allows you to sample popular dishes such as squid ink gnocchi, tortellini stuffed with cannellini beans, and, of course, the obligatory chorizo stuffed squid.
- Be sure to try one of mixologist Benjamin Schiller's seafood appropriate drinks, including a great Dark and Stormy.

Leopold

Belgian   www.leopoldchicago.com
1450 West Chicago Avenue   @leopoldchicago
Chicago, IL 60622
312.348.1028

- Chef Jeffrey Hedin (Witt's Tavern, Blue Water Grill, Green Zebra) creates a Belgian inspired menu providing many of the classics, as well as modern interpretations of some Belgian dishes.
- Hedin describes his cooking as "simple and seasonal" and offers a menu that changes seasonally and highlights produce from many of the area's local farms.
- Classic fare is represented here, with moules frites, poutine, and steak tartare capped with a raw egg yolk, and smoked rabbit leg with mustard spaetzle.

Maude's Liquor Bar

Coastal French   www.maudesliquorbar.com
840 West Randolph Street   @MaudesChicago
Chicago, IL 60607
312.243.9712

- A collaboration between executive chef Jeff Pikus (Alinea, Gilt Bar) and Brendan Sodikoff (Gilt Bar), Maude's Liquor Bar is a French Bistro that inhabits the world between a restaurant and a bar, and does so while providing a cool vibe.
- With strong seafood offerings, be sure to try the oysters, with varieties from both the east and west coast offered nightly.
- If you prefer more classic French fare, Maude's also has roasted bone marrow, steak tartare topped with a yolk, and foie gras torchon, as well as a variety of other offerings.

Next

Various   www.nextrestaurant.com
953 West Fulton Market   @NextRestaurant
Chicago, IL 60607
312. 226.0858

- Chef Dave Beran and co-owner Grant Achatz received universal praise from the Chicago culinary community by creating a unique dining experience that borders on theater.
- Eschewing reservations, Next instead relies on a lottery ticket system in which you register on their website and are notified when tickets become available. Tickets sell out within seconds for this 62 seat restaurant, so act fast.
- The menu changes four times a year, and each menu features a particular theme, such as "Paris 1906," "A Tour of Thailand," and "Sicily."

Owen & Engine

British Gastropub
2700 North Western Avenue
Chicago, IL 60647
773. 235.2930

www.owenandengine.com
@OwenandEngine

- Chef Charles Burkhardt brings authentic British comfort food to Chicago, with classic British décor to match. Dark wood, fireplaces, and leather club chairs might make you feel like you're in a British Members Club.
- The Haddock for the fish and chips is flown in daily from Georges Bank in the North Atlantic, while the bangers and mash, fresh lamb sausage, and the Cornish pasty will make you feel like you're across the pond in jolly old England.
- The charcuterie plate has been called the "must have" dish to order, with liver pate, pork rillets and sausage.

Ruxbin Kitchen

American Bistro
851 North Ashland Avenue
Chicago, IL 60642
312. 624.8509

www.ruxbinchicago.com
@RuxbinChicago

- Chef Edward Kim (Per Se) combines French technique studied at Le Cordon Bleu with his Asian heritage and other influences to create a menu that is inventive, yet approachable.
- With only six main courses, the chef has received rave reviews for his K-town empanadas, pan-seared trout fillet, and hanger steak with cauliflower purée.
- You might feel like you've stepped into a salvage shop, as the décor makes use of recycled, repurposed materials, such as walls made from apple juice shipping crates.

Vera

Spanish Wine Bar   www.verachicago.com
1023 West Lake Street   @VeraChicago
Chicago, IL 60607
312.243.9770

- Chef Mark Mendez and his sommelier wife Elizabeth, both formerly of Carnivale, have decided to scale things down for their own restaurant, focusing on small, simple dishes and wines from Spain.
- While the plates may be small, the food looms large here, with black cod fillet, beef-stuffed potato croquette, Iberico ham, and paella with duck chorizo and pieces of rabbit fulfilling the chef's mission to get back to his roots.
- Most everything on the menu is under $12, except for the paella, which can easily feed two people.

For a complete list of Chicago food resources, visit kundaeats.com/chicago.

24

Jean-Robert's Table

French   www.jrtable.com
713 Vine Street   @jrtable
Cincinnati, OH 45202
513.621.4777

- Master Chef Jean-Robert de Cavel (The Maisonette, Jean-Robert at Pigall's) is one of less than 60 French Master Chefs in North America, and is also the recipient of the Medal of the Chevalier de l'ordre du Merite (one of France's highest honors).
- Cavel's latest restaurant allows him to showcase centuries of French culinary tradition, while bringing his own contemporary sensibility, all in a casually elegant setting.
- Utilizing classic French technique paired with local, seasonal ingredients, Cavel offers classic creations like foie gras, fried frog legs and snails, skate fish wings, and 3 little cochon.

For a complete list of Cincinnati food resources, visit kundaeats.com/cincinnati.

25

Deagan's Kitchen & Bar

Gastropub   www.deagans.com
14810 Detroit Avenue   @DeagansKitchen
Lakewood, OH 44107
216.767.5775

- Owner Dan Deagan and chef Demetrios Atheneos (Giovanni's, Bella Lucca, Bodega) understand the proper concept of a "gastropub" and get it right, by combining top notch cuisine with craft beer in an informal, casual setting.
- Atheneos' menu is creative and the dishes are well prepared, with items like Amish chicken and waffles, lobster & cheese, and the gastropub staple, fish and chips.
- The "pub" portion of this gastropub is well represented, as it features 28 craft beers on draft.

Ginko

Japanese-Sushi Bar   www.restaurantdante.us
2247 Professor Avenue   @danteboccuzzi
Cleveland, OH 44113
216.274.1200

- The vibrancy of Tokyo comes to Cleveland, as noted chef/restaurateur, Dante Boccuzzi (Nobu, Aureole, Dante), brings his new, authentic sushi bar to the city.
- Located in the former Third Federal Savings and Loan building, Ginko features a concrete bar with a flowing river sealed under glass, and TV's that show Japanese anime.
- Head chef, Taishi Noma, born in Kyoto, follows the authentic Japanese approach by focusing attention on the fish, which is flown in daily from Japan, Hawaii and New York.

For a complete list of Cleveland food resources, visit kundaeats.com/cleveland.

Good 2 Go Taco

Mexican   www.good2gotaco.com
1146 Peavy Road   @good2gotaco
Dallas, TX 75218
214.519.9110

- Good 2 Go Taco has graduated from their original Green Spot gas station stand to a permanent storefront on Peavy and Garland.
- Co-owners Jeana Johnson and Colleen O'Hare (Green Room, Stephan Pyles) elevate the humble taco by using haute flavor combinations and clever names.
- The menu rotates frequently with examples like "Holy Mole" (braised goat in mole with black beans, verde rice and chipotle cheddar) and "The Fredo" (roasted spring onions, red peppers, crimini mushrooms, Parmesan potatoes, fresh spinach). Related burrito combinations are also available.

Il Cane Rosso

Pizza   www.ilcanerosso.com
2612 Commerce Street   @canerosso
Dallas, TX 75226
214.741.1188

- Escaping the corporate world, owner Jay Jerrier received his pizza epiphany during a vacation to Italy.
- Baked in a Stefano Ferrara wood-burning oven, Il Cane Rosso's pies hold the rare certification from the Associazone Verace Pizza Napoletana.
- The restaurant means "Red Dog" in Italian, a tribute to Jerrier's first dog.

Lucia

Italian   www.luciadallas.com
408 West Eighth Street   @LuciaDallas
Dallas, TX 75208
214.948.4998

- Located in the Bishop Arts District, Lucia specializes in multi-Provincial Italian dishes with an emphasis on hand-cured meats (salami, soppressata, pancetta tesa) and scratch pastas (gnocchi, cappellacci, farro verde).
- Organized in the classic antipasti, primi, secondi, dolci trattoria format, chef David Uygur's menu refreshes constantly as he explores the entire universe of pasta.
- Uygur's wife, Jennifer, curates the wine program with an obvious emphasis on Italian varietals.

Mesa Veracruz Coastal Cuisine

Coastal-Mexican   www.mesadallas.com
118 West Jefferson Boulevard   @MESA59
Dallas, TX 75208
214.941.4246

- Chef-Owners Raul and Olga Reyes bring the unique flavors of their hometown Alvarado, Veracruz Mexico to the lone star state.
- Coastal "Del Mar" Mexican dishes stand out, particularly, the seafood melodies of arroz ala tumbala (shrimp, scallops, mussels, crab and octopus) and chilpachol de jaiba y camaron (crab, Gulf shrimp, masa dumplings mussels).
- The signature mole in the Mama Cata duck is based on a family recipe compromising of over 20 ingredients.

Shinjuku Station

Japanese-Izakaya   www.shinjuku-station.com
711 West Magnolia Avenue
Fort Worth, TX 76104
817.923.2695

- This izakaya grabbed the attention of the Magnolia Avenue dining scene with its creative renditions of Japanese bar food and sushi.
- The Fort Worth critics were particularly enamored with the okonomiyaki plate, aka Japanese pizza (pork belly, cabbage, kizame shoga).
- Multi-course omakase dinners with sake parings are available by reservation or special occasions.
- Shinjuku Station is named after the busiest train station in Japan.

For a complete list of Dallas food resources, visit kundaeats.com/dallas.

Bittersweet

New American   www.bittersweetdenver.com
500 East Alameda Avenue   @dinebittersweet
Denver, CO 80209
303.942.0320

- Chef Olav Peterson (Bistro One, 1515) realizes a lifelong dream with his new restaurant, taking an artisanal old world approach to rustic cuisine with modern touches.
- Peterson has over 600 sq ft of garden space at the restaurant, and in spring, the organic garden will grow much of the seasonal produce featured in the menu.
- As befits the artisanal approach, breads, pastas and desserts are house made and meats are house cured.
- The menu is seasonal and changes regularly, but expect to find rustic dishes like sweetbread reuben, halibut cheeks with fried oysters, ox tail, and vegetable shepherd's pie.

ChoLon Modern Asian Bistro

Southeast Asian   www.cholon.com
1555 Blake Street   @ChoLonBistro
Denver, CO 80202
303.353.5223

- Chef/owner Lon Symensma (Jean Georges Shanghai, Spice Market, Buddakan) spent a year traveling throughout Southeast Asia and China, and puts the knowledge he gained to good use at ChoLon Bistro.
- Symensma's menu features inspired interpretations of traditional Asian dishes with his own unique twists.
- The vibrant flavors of Asia are showcased in dishes like Singapore style lobster, pork belly pot stickers, and Pho bo.

Linger

Global Street Food
2030 West 30th Avenue
Denver, CO 80211
303.993.3120

www.lingerdenver.com
@LingerDenver

- Housed in a former mortuary, you'll be dying to eat at chef-owner Justin Cucci's (Root Down) new "eatuary" with stunning views of downtown Denver and an exciting global menu to match.
- Cucci traveled the world to get ideas for his menu, focusing on global street food from every continent, while providing his own unique twists where necessary.
- The menu is organized by geographic region, and the small plate approach allows you to mix and match various regional tastes, such as Mongolian BBQ duck buns, masala dosa, Turkish chile, and raw, vegan Indian samosas.

The Pullman

Farm-to-Table
330 7th Street
Glenwood Springs, CO 81601
970.230.9234

www.thepullmangws.com
@thePullmanGWS

- The Pullman is the newest restaurant from chef-owner Mark Fischer (Six89), who is gaining a reputation for revitalizing communities and turning them into culinary destinations.
- A James Beard semifinalist, Fischer espouses a "Farm-to-Table" philosophy at his new restaurant and relies on fresh, seasonal ingredients from local purveyors.
- Dishes that have received praise include pierogi with caramelized onions, roast Colorado bass, roast bone marrow, and Colorado lamb shoulder with lemon risotto.

TAG | RAW BAR

Raw Food   www.tagrawbar.com
1423 Larimer Street, Suite 010   @TAG_RAW_BAR_CO
Denver, CO 80202
303.996.2685

- TAG Raw Bar is an interesting new concept from the mind of owner Troy Guard (Nine75), with the goal of creating simple and delicious meals that won't weigh you down.
- Chef Samuel Freund (One If By Land, Two If By Sea, TAG) develops his cuisine by using fresh, seasonal ingredients from their rawest form. No item is heated with more than a torch.
- The light menu is filled with raw dishes such as ceviche, raw fish taco, ahi jalapeno, and a variety of salads and fresh sushi.

For a complete list of Denver food resources, visit kundaeats.com/denver.

32

Mani Osteria & Bar

Italian   www.maniosteria.com
341 East Liberty   @ManiOsteriaBar
Ann Arbor, MI 48104
734.769.6700

- Appropriately, Mani means "hand-made" in Italian.
- The Ann-Arbor restaurant specializes in antipasti small plates, wood-oven artisanal pizzas, and homemade pasta dishes.
- The Proscuitto Flight is pork heaven featuring a hat trick of Prosciutto di Parma, Jamon Serrano and American La Quercia Proscuitto.

The Root Restaurant & Bar

New American   www.therootrestaurant.com
340 Town Center Boulevard
White Lake, MI 48386
248.698.2400

- Owners Ed Mamou and James Rigato are on a quest to find the "root of great food and dining and eliminating that which is not." Those roots lie firmly in Michigan terra firma.
- The end result is a made-from-scratch, seasonal menu leveraging regional ingredients from local purveyors.
- Detroit diners are making the commute to White Lake Township to try dishes like Spicer's Cider (local) braised Michigan pork and farm-raised Michigan shrimp in Guernsey Farms cream sauce (local). Wash it all down with an all Michigan draft beer list.

Sterling's Bistro

American Bistro   www.sterlingsbistro.com
13905 Lakeside Circle
Sterling Heights, MI 48313
586.566.0627

- Sterling Heights diners welcomed Sterling's Bistro from day one, thanks to a great "bang for your buck" menu.
- Favorite dishes include mussels Rockefeller, herb encrusted prime rib, and goat cheese fondue. Try not to spoil your appetite with the addictive flatbreads that are baked on location in a brick-hearth oven.
- The wine list is massive, and martinis are the signature drink

For a complete list of Detroit food resources, visit kundaeats.com/detroit.

3800 Ocean

Seafood-New American   www.3800oceanrestaurant.com
3800 North Ocean Drive
Singer Island, FL 33404
561.340.1795

- Residing within the Palm Beach Marriott Singer Island Beach Resort & Spa, 3800 Ocean boasts American regional cuisine using the finest local and seasonal ingredients, with a beautiful oceanfront view. Outdoor patio dining is available.
- Using a "collective kitchen" approach with a team of chefs, each chef brings a new insight to the table, offering regional flavors from New England, Mexico, Jamaica, and Long Island.
- The menu offers such items as "Mojo" marinated pork tenderloin, Ingrid's New England day boat scallops, seared yellowfin tuna, and grilled filet mignon.

Buccan

New American-Tapas   www.buccanpalmbeach.com
350 South County Road   @buccanpalmbeach
Palm Beach, FL 33480
561.833.3450

- Sophisticated cuisine comes to Palm Beach with the arrival of chef Clay Conley's (Azul) new restaurant, named for the Caribbean wooden grill used to cook food over open fire.
- Conley focuses on the freshest ingredients available at the market, and changes his menu daily and weekly, according to what's available at the moment.
- Using the small plate approach to allow sharing a variety of options, Conley offers dishes like squid ink orecchiette, shrimp dumplings, and a much praised steak tartare.

Rok:Brgr

Burger Bar-Gastropub   www.rokbrgr.com
208 Southwest 2nd Street
Fort Lauderdale, FL 33301
954.525.7656

- Giving off the vibe of a 1920's era prohibition bar in the historic Himmarshee District, Rok:Brgr is a gourmet burger bar and gastropub that takes a modern approach on American comfort foods.
- Chef Robyn Martinez provides you with the ultimate burger experience, with over 17 signature burgers and a "create your own burger" section.
- The menu features other comfort foods as well, like mac and cheese, homemade fish and chips, and lobster corn dogs.
- Vegetarians will enjoy the veggie burger and salads.

Verdea Restaurant & Wine Bar

Farm-to-Table   www.verdearestaurant.com
4350 PGA Boulevard
Palm Beach Gardens, FL 33410
561.691.3130

- Located in the Embassy Suites in Palm Beach Gardens, Verdea Restaurant & Wine Bar is a sleek new restaurant offering contemporary Farm-to-Table cuisine.
- Chef David Welch's (Smith & Wollensky, Tantra, Acqualina) style can be described as contemporary and tropical, based on regional fresh fruit and seafood.
- The menu is seasonal, with dishes like acorn squash, duo of duck, milk fed veal chop, and crusted black grouper.

For a complete list of Fort Lauderdale food resources, visit kundaeats.com/fortlauderdale.

Bricco Trattoria

Italian   www.billygrant.com
124 Hebron Avenue
Glastonbury, CT 06033
860.659.0220

- Bricco Trattoria delivers their traditional Italian farm house and enoteca concept to Glastonbury.
- Though the menu changes daily, popular dishes like salumi antipasti, ribeye for two, and wood-oven pizzas are staples.
- Hartford legend and restaurant owner Billy Grant's (Bricco, Grants) motto is "Eat And Live Well Always."

For a complete list of Hartford food resources, visit kundaeats.com/hartford.

Brasserie 19

French   www.brasserie19.com
1962 West Gray Street   @brasserie19
Houston, TX 77019
713.524.1919

- This quintessential French brasserie in the 77019 neighborhood is the brainchild of Charles Clark and Grant Cooper (Catalan).
- Helmed by veteran executive chef Mark Schmidt (The Rainbow Lodge, Café 909, AquaKnox), the menu features France's greatest hits: everything from frog legs and foie gras to Dover sole and cassoulet.
- Friendly, "just above retail" wine prices are a signature feature of all Clark Cooper Concepts.

El Gran Malo

Gastrocantina   www.elgranmalo.com
2307 Ella Boulevard   @elgranmalotx
Houston, Texas 77008
832.767.3405

- El Gran Malo is a "gastrocantina" featuring craft tequila cocktails and a Tex-Mex small plates menu designed by chef Greg Lowry.
- Translation: The Big Bad. We're not sure whether that refers to the margaritas or the infamous Torta burger with fried egg, chorizo, and pork belly.
- Six types of tacos (snapper, shrimp, pork carnitas, chicken tinga, beef, Mexican Coca Cola-braised pork belly) with choice of clever toppings are available in lots of three.

Mala Sichuan

Chinese-Sichuan   Search Facebook
9348 Bellaire Boulevard
Houston, TX 77036
713.995.1889

- Billed as a "second generation" Chinatown restaurant, Mala Sichuan serves authentic Sichuanese cuisine with an updated approach.
- True to its namesake (Ma means "Numbing "and La means "Spicy"), owner Cori Xiong leads an all-Sichuan trained team of chefs as they explore the spicy peppercorn sauce dishes made famous by the region (e.g., Dan Dan noodles and Couple's Lung Slices offal).
- Live Tilapia fish tanks on-site ensure aquarium-to-table freshness.

Pondicheri Café

Indian   www.pondichericafe.com
2800 Kirby Drive   @pondicheri
Houston, TX 77098
713.522.2022

- Combining traditional flavors with locally-sourced ingredients (think Gulf Coast Shrimp Chaat), Pondicheri serves enlightened Indian street food/baked goods from breakfast-to-dinner.
- The restaurant has embraced the environmentally responsible practice, made famous in Mumbai, of re-usable, exchangeable Pondi food containers.
- Owner Anita Jaisinghani (Indika) was honored twice by the Beard Foundation garnering nominations for Best New Restaurant and Best Southwest Chef.

Radical Eats

Vegetarian-Mexican
3903 Fulton Street
Houston, TX 77009
713.697.8719

www.radicaleats.com
@radicaleats

- This north side Houston Heights restaurant is most famous for their vegan tamales and "kick ass vegetarian Mexican" menu.
- Radical Eats advocates the healthy benefits of a plants-only, gluten-free, preservative-free diet.
- Owner-chef and cancer survivor, Staci Davis (Basil's), gained fame in the late eighties as a caterer for vegetarian rock bands (10,000 Maniacs, Love and Rockets, Psychedelic Furs) visiting Houston.

Tango & Malbec

South American
2800 Sage Road
Houston, TX 77056
713.629.8646

www.tangomalbec.com

- Traditional meat dishes (bife de lomo, costillitas de cordero, chicken Milanesas) from Argentina and Uruguay are cooked the old country way on a custom-made wood grill.
- A large selection of the eponymous malbec wines pairs well with the Rioplatense menu of chef Mariela Hecker.
- Yes, live tango on the weekends.

For a complete list of Houston food resources, visit kundaeats.com/houston.

The Indigo Duck
Southern-French   www.theindigoduck.com
39 East Court Street   @TheIndigoDuck
Franklin, IN 46131
317.560.5805

- Having grown up in Charleston, SC, chef Joseph Hewett (Oakleys Bistro, Richard's Kitchen) seamlessly blends his Southern upbringing with formal culinary training to offer Southern soul food with classical French technique.
- Working with local farmers, fishermen, and purveyors, Hewett focuses on fresh, seasonal ingredients.
- While the menu is seasonal and changes accordingly, expect to find signature dishes such as shrimp and grits, maple-spiced duck breast, and pecan crusted pork loin.

Mesh on Mass
New American   www.meshonmass.com
725 Massachusetts Avenue   @CRG_Mesh
Indianapolis, IN 46204
317.955.9600

- Mesh on Mass is the latest entrant from Cunningham Restaurant Group (Charbonos, Café 251) to the downtown Indianapolis gastronomic scene.
- Keeping things simple, Mesh on Mass still manages to offer a creative menu diverse enough to sate a variety of appetites.
- The menu offers items from land and sea, such as Cuban chicken, grilled Colorado lamb, jumbo lump crab cakes, and crab crusted salmon.

For a complete list of Indianapolis food resources, visit kundaeats.com/indianapolis.

Beer Kitchen No. 1

Gastropub   www.beerkitchenkc.com
435 Westport Road
Kansas City, MO 64111
816.389.4180

- The new gastropub from owners Mark Kelpe and James Westphal (The Foundry, McCoy's Public House, One80) is a decided change in concept from the restaurant it replaces.
- More "rough and tumble" than upscale, Beer Kitchen No. 1 offers a casual, easy going atmosphere with music.
- In addition to the usual gastropub fare, such as oven fried chicken, and fish & chips, healthy vegetarian options like vegetarian meatloaf and shepherd's pie are also offered.

The Rieger Hotel Grill & Exchange

New American   www.theriegerkc.com
1924 Main Street   @TheRieger
Kansas City, MO 64108
816.471.2177

- Chef/owner Howard Hanna's (River Club, Room 39) new restaurant is set in the historic Rieger Hotel, which opened in 1915 and has a deep, rich history in Kansas City.
- With the belief that rich culinary traditions were formed in medium sized cities, in the heartland of various countries, Hanna sets out to prove it with a local, seasonal menu that is rustic and soulful and celebrates the bounty of the region.
- Bringing modern technique to classic American cuisine, the chef creates a seasonal menu with rabbit potpie, Rieger pork soup, and filet of rainbow trout.

For a complete list of Kansas City food resources, visit kundaeats.com/kansascity.

Gosh Ethiopian Restaurant

Ethiopian   www.goshethiopian.com
3609 Sutherland Avenue   @goshethiopian
Knoxville, TN 37919
865.544.4475

- Finally, the city of Knoxville gets its first Ethiopian restaurant, and it lives up to the expectations, delivering authentic Ethiopian cuisine in a casual, simple environment.
- For the unadventurous, don't worry. The owner, Tariku, is gracious and willing to explain the cuisine to help you decide what to order.
- Ethiopian cuisine eschews the use of silverware and utensils, instead relying on delicious injera, a traditional flat bread that is used to scoop up the various meat and vegetable stews. At Gosh, even the plate is edible!

Jacque's Whistle Stop Cafe

BBQ   www.jacquesbbq.com
110 West College Street
Friendsville, TN 37737
865.980.3322

- For a taste of authentic southern BBQ, take a trip off the beaten path, and make a stop at Jacque's Whistle Stop Café, a unique combination of antique store/restaurant.
- Owner-BBQ chef Jacqúe Pierre, AKA Donald Pierce, has been making and selling his own brand of BBQ sauce for years, and now you can sample it on the 1/2 chargrilled chicken, 1/2 rack of ribs, and the London broiled sandwich.
- Peruse the antiques for sale while waiting for your order.

For a complete list of Knoxville food resources, visit kundaeats.com/knoxville.

Comme Ça

French Bistro   www.commecarestaurant.com
3708 Las Vegas Boulevard South   @chefdavidmyers
Las Vegas, NV 89109
702.698.7910

- Located in The Cosmopolitan of Las Vegas, chef/founder David Myers' (Les Crayères, Daniel, Sona) new restaurant offers authentic French bistro cuisine.
- While the food may be authentic bistro fare, don't expect the restaurant itself to look exactly like a French bistro, as Myers goes for a more fun, amusing vibe, with chalkboards for walls and a giant map showing his favorite restaurants in France.
- The menu offers traditional dishes with the freshest locally farmed ingredients, such as roasted chicken with ratatouille, moules frites, and crispy skate lyonnaise.

Crab Corner

Seafood   www.nvseafood.com
4161 South Eastern Avenue   @CrabCorner
Las Vegas, NV 89119
702.489.4646

- Hailing from Bowie, Maryland, owners-operators Mark and John Smolen started out by distributing live product to a variety of grocery stores and restaurants.
- After repeated requests, they decided to provide their retail customers with an authentic crab house like they had in Maryland, and seafood lovers in Las Vegas can be thankful.
- Live female and male Blue Crabs are sourced from the Chesapeake Bay and its tributaries and are flown in daily and delivered to you within 24 hours of coming out of the water.

Jaleo

Spanish Tapas   www.jaleo.com
3708 Las Vegas Boulevard South   @JaleoLasVegas
Las Vegas, NV 89109
702.698.7950

- James Beard's 2011 Outstanding Chef of the Year winner, José Andrés (minibar by josé andrés, Zaytinya, Oyamel), is regarded as the father of the tapas movement in America.
- Jaleo means "revelry" in Spanish, and the restaurant lives up to its name, providing a fun, festive, casual environment.
- Under the direction of Andrés, Jaleo offers an assortment of tapas, the traditional small dishes of Spain, which are meant to be shared and enjoyed with others in a communal manner.
- With almost 70 items to choose from, be sure to try the famous paella and save room for the Spanish flan.

For a complete list of Las Vegas food resources, visit kundaeats.com/lasvegas.

45

Manhattan Beach Post

New American   www.eatmbpost.com
1142 Manhattan Avenue   @ChefDLeFevre
Manhattan Beach, CA 90266
310.545.5405

- Chef-owner David LeFevre (Charlie Trotter's, Water Grill) creates a neighborhood "Social House" in Manhattan Beach with a lively, engaging, and relaxed atmosphere.
- The rustic menu made up of small, shared plate dishes articulates LeFevre's globetrotting experiences by blending influences from Morocco, Provence, Japan, Spain, China and more.
- Braised hog jowl, grilled sword squid, braised lamb belly, and buttermilk biscuits with bacon and cheddar are just some of the unique "must have" creations on the menu.

Mezze

Middle Eastern   www.mezzela.com
401 North La Cienega Boulevard   @MEZZE_LA
Los Angeles, CA 90048
310.657.4103

- Chef Micah Wexler (Craft, L'Atelier de Joël Robuchon, Voyeur) fuses the influences of the Middle East, including Lebanon, Syria, Morocco and Turkey, in his new restaurant named after the Middle Eastern version of shared plates (think tapas).
- Your palate will taste the spices with presentations of braised tripe with falafel balls, flatbread topped with Armenian sausage, chopped chicken livers, and wood-roasted baby chicken.

Ombra Ristorante

Italian   www.ombrala.com
3737 Cahuenga Boulevard   @OmbraLA
Studio City, CA 91604
818.985.7337

- Named for the Italian term for ordering wine by the glass, Ombra Ristorante is chef-owner Michael J. Young's new vision to provide the experience of a local restaurant in Venice.
- The menu is seasonal and is changed every few months.
- As you would expect, authenticity is evident throughout, with wild boar meatballs, lamb chops in yoghurt sauce, and braised brisket providing the Italian experience.
- The décor is simple, with sound panels added to reduce noise.

Picca

Peruvian   www.piccaperu.com
9575 West Pico Boulevard   @PiccaPeru
Los Angeles, CA 90035
310.277.0133

- Chef Ricardo Zarate was named Best New Chef in America by Food & Wine Magazine in 2011. He lives up to that accolade with his latest restaurant, creating modern Peruvian cuisine with a Japanese influence.
- Sit at the Chef's counter and watch him and his team create wonderful dishes like beef heart on a pair of skewers, duck leg confit in black beer sauce over cilantro rice, and roasted black cod over sun-dried potato stew.
- Picca means "to nibble" and that's what you'll want to do.

Ray's & Stark Bar

Mediterranean
5905 Wilshire Boulevard
Los Angeles, CA 90036
323.857.6180

www.patinagroup.com
@RaysandStarkBar

- Why not get a little culture with your food? Ray's & Stark Bar is located in the Los Angeles County Museum of Art, and was designed by famed architect Renzo Piano.
- Chef Kris Morningstar (District, Blue Velvet) has created a Mediterranean-inspired menu with a farm-to-table, seasonal focus.
- Depending on the season, you'll find creations such as wild red king salmon confit, lamb sweetbreads with artichokes, wild striped bass, and hanger steak with smoked marrow.
- The restaurant is named for noted film producer, Ray Stark.

Red Medicine

Vietnamese Fusion
8400 Wilshire Boulevard
Beverly Hills, CA 90211
323.651.5500

www.redmedicinela.com
@redmedicinela

- "This is not a traditional Vietnamese restaurant"… says Chef-co-owner Jordan Kahn (French Laundry, Per se, Alinea, Michael Mina). Instead, Kahn distills the essence of Vietnamese cuisine into creations that will challenge your perception of Asian cuisine.
- Dishes such as bánh mì, dungeness crab, heirloom rice porridge, and pork rillette maintain the essence of Vietnam while incorporating Kahn's unique twists.
- The idea for Red Medicine was born during many late, late night Asian meals after long hours working at restaurants.

The Royce at the Langham

New American-French   www.roycela.com
1401 South Oak Knoll Avenue   @RoyceLA
Pasadena, CA 91106
626.585.6410

- Chef David Féau grew up in France and honed his skills at some of the best restaurants in the country (Bistrot de L'Etoile, Le Miravile) and learned under the guidance of famed chef Guy Savoy.
- Féau was named one of the Six Best Chefs in France Under 30 Years Old by Le Chef Magazine.
- The menu is comprised of lighter California fare prepared with classic French influences, emphasizing fresh seasonal produce and the best quality products from around the world.

Son of a Gun

Seafood   www.sonofagunrestaurant.com
8370 West 3rd Street
Los Angeles, CA 90048
323.782.9033

- Chefs-owners, Jon Shook and Vinny Dotolo, of Animal restaurant fame, bring a Florida Keys fish house vibe to Hollywood with their latest establishment.
- Fresh seafood is the specialty here, with oysters on the half shell, smoked steelhead roe, and Brandade (salt cod with potatoes) on the menu. But if you prefer more "land based" food, try the fried chicken sandwich or the Benton's country ham.
- The authentic vintage maritime décor looks like it could have come out of Quint's shack in "Jaws".

Sotto

Southern Italian   www.sottorestaurant.com
9575 West Pico Boulevard   @sottoLA
Los Angeles, CA 90035
310.277.0210

- Chefs Steve Samson and Zach Pollack, who worked together at Test Kitchen, Sona, and Pizzeria Ortica, focus on regional cuisine from Southern Italy.
- Both Samson and Pollack worked at some of the top restaurants in Italy and, thankfully, brought back some of the authentic, rustic, lesser known dishes with them to LA.
- Dishes such as braised lamb ragu, buckwheat pasta with pig's head sauce, squid ink fusilli, and braised octopus tentacles highlight the chefs' commitment to authentic cuisine.

For a complete list of Los Angeles food resources, visit kundaeats.com/losangeles.

50

Doc Crows Southern Smokehouse & Raw Bar

Southern   www.doccrows.com
127 West Main Street   @DocCrows
Louisville, KY 40202
502.587.1626

- Situated in historic Whiskey Row, and named after the inventor of the sour mash process, Doc Crow's is the latest restaurant from brothers Steven and Michael Ton (Basa).
- Chef Michael Ton (Olive, Basa) creates a menu focused on traditional southern cooking, with long time southern favorites like po-boys, pork chops, and baby back ribs.
- Master Sommelier/owner Brett Davis is one of only 102 master whisky sommeliers in the country.

Harvest

Classic American Farm-to-Table   www.harvestlouisville.com
624 East Market Street   @Harvest502
Louisville, KY 40202
502.384.9090

- Harvest is a new restaurant from Ivor Chodkowski (Bardstown Road Farmer's Market), the man who helped foster the "Farm-to-Table" advancement in Louisville.
- Harvest's goal is to source the vast majority of its ingredients from within 100 miles of the city.
- Chef Coby Ming showcases local ingredients in traditional dishes like hog jowl muffins, buttermilk fried chicken, and pork shoulder.

For a complete list of Louisville food resources, visit kundaeats.com/louisville.

Tempest Oyster Bar

Seafood   www.tempestoyster.com
120 East Wilson Street
Madison, WI 53703
608.258.1443

- With a 1948 Chris Craft boat in the dining room, and a large blue marlin mounted on the wall, owner Henry Doane's (Tornado Steak House, Orpheum) new fresh seafood restaurant is a welcome addition to Madison's dining scene.
- The predominantly seafood menu, created by Chef Greg Walters, is all sustainably sourced and delivered fresh to the restaurant.
- Yellowfin tuna, pan-fried flounder, and the highly touted fish and chips share menu space with non-seafood items such as venison chops, and bone-in strip steaks.

For a complete list of Madison food resources, visit kundaeats.com/madison.

52

Acre

New American   www.acrememphis.com
690 South Perkins
Memphis, TN 38117
901.818.2273

- Chef Wally Joe (KC's, Wally Joe) was born in Hong Kong and raised in the Mississippi Delta. He was taught at a young age to commune with nature and learn about the "roots" of food.
- Joe uses the absolute best products available and does as little as possible to them, allowing each ingredient to shine.
- The menu seamlessly combines hints of Italy, Asia and the American South all deeply rooted in classical French techniques. The results include dishes like dungeness crab cake, truffle studded chicken, and rabbit "coppa."

The Elegant Farmer

New American Farm-to-Table   www.theelegantfarmerrestaurant.com
262 South Highland Street   @elegantfarmertn
Memphis, TN 38111
901.324.2221

- The Elegant Farmer is chef-owner Mac Edwards' (McEwen's on Monroe) latest restaurant and his goal is to bring you his interpretation of "elevated" comfort food by using the freshest regional ingredients from sustainable farms.
- Edwards was a past Memphis Restaurant Association "Restaurateur of the Year" winner.
- Sourcing his ingredients from local and regional farmers and purveyors, Edwards crafts a traditional menu with farm raised redfish, country fried steak, and old school salmon patties.

Sweet Grass Next Door

Southern Coastal-Bar   www.sweetgrassmemphis.com
937 South Cooper Street   @SweetGrassMem
Memphis, TN 38104
901.278.0278

- Located in the space next door to the larger Sweet Grass restaurant, Sweet Grass Next Door is a casual bistro offering a limited, but no less exciting menu.
- Chef Ryan Trimm's new restaurant offers Low Country style cuisine with local ingredients in a casual, laid back environment.
- Some of Sweetgrass' regular menu items can be found here as well.
- Dishes include chicken and waffles, shrimp and grits, fried egg sandwich, and macaroni and cheese croquette.

For a complete list of Memphis food resources, visit kundaeats.com/memphis.

1500 Degrees

Steak House   www.1500degreesmiami.com
4525 Collins Avenue
Miami Beach, FL 33140
305.674.5594

- Best described as a farm-to-table steakhouse and raw bar, 1500° is the flagship restaurant of Miami Beach's Eden Roc Renaissance Hotel.
- Chef Paula DaSilva (3030) made her bones by winning runner-up in Gordon Ramsay's "Hell's Kitchen" television show.
- Seared grass-fed steaks can be paired with a dizzying selection of over 20 different farm-fresh sides and sauces/butter.

Makoto

Japanese   www.makoto-restaurant.com
9700 Collins Avenue #107   @Makoto_BH
Bal Harbour, FL 33154
305.864.8600

- Joining a very competitive Miami market, Beard winning chef Makoto Okuwa (Morimoto, Sashi Sushi and Sake Lounge) partners with Stephen Starr on this Bal Harbour Japanese project.
- Though master itamae-crafted sushi is the obvious focus of Makoto, the all American hamburger with tempura sides has developed a cult following.
- Okuwa once competed against Michael Symon on Iron Chef in a sea urchin challenge.

Pubbelly

Asian Gastropub
1418 20th Street
Miami Beach, FL 33139
305.532.7555

www.pubbelly.com
@pubbelly

- Pubbelly Sushi is part of the Andreas Schreiner, Jose Mendin (Nobu) & Sergio Navarro restaurant triad.
- The no-reservations South Beach gastropub features ambitious fusion sushi and re-imagined Asian Street food small plates (dumplings, noodles, pork buns).
- Top shelf sake paired with craft ingredients (e.g., tamarind, maracuya, ginger, lychee, chiles, rosé) are the pub standards.

Yardbird

Southern
1600 Lenox Avenue
Miami Beach, FL 33139
305.538.5220

www.runchickenrun.com
@yardbird

- Yardbird Southern Table & Bar specializes in Southern fare with staples like shrimp n' grits, pimento cheese, and fried green tomatoes.
- However, it's the brined fried chicken that has made Miamians flock to Chef Jeff McInnis' temple of Dixie. Llewellyn's Fine Fried Chicken with cheddar and chow chow waffle, Tupelo honey, and citrus watermelon salad takes over 27 hours to prepare.
- Not surprisingly, straight bourbon and mason jar bourbon cocktails dominate the bar menu with over 40 choices including Pappy Van Winkle.

Zuma Japanese Restaurant

Japanese   www.zumarestaurant.com
270 Biscayne Boulevard Way
Miami, FL 33131
305.577.0277

- This haute izakaya is an outpost of the original London location considered one of the best restaurants in the world.
- Located inside downtown Miami's Epic Hotel, the modern first floor lobby space features a sushi and robata bar overlooking the Miami River.
- The Japanese small plates menu is broken up into four main sections: robata grill, tempura, sushi, and the signature dishes (kinoko no kama meshi rice bowl, rib eye no daikon ponzu fumi, and lobster no oven yaki).

For a complete list of Miami food resources, visit kundaeats.com/miami.

Beta by Sabor

Brazilian Churrascaria   www.saborbrazil.net
777 North Water Street   @BetaBySabor
Milwaukee, WI 53202
414.431.3106

- Uniquely located within another restaurant, which happens to be a Brazilian churrascaria, Beta by Sabor is a gastropub that follows the popular small plate philosophy.
- Chef Mitch Ciohon delivers unique flavors that will leave a big impression.
- Standout items include roasted beef bone marrow, braised veal and halibut cheeks, chicken and waffles, and pork ragout.
- The prices are in keeping with the small plate philosophy, with most dishes under $13.
- Save room for the Ice cream, which is whipped up tableside in an impressive cloud of liquid nitrogen.

The Rumpus Room

British Gastropub   www.rumpusroommke.com
1030 North Water Street   @bartolottas
Milwaukee, WI 53202
414.292.0100

- The latest venture from the Bartolotta Restaurant Group, The Rumpus Room brings a British gastropub to Milwaukee, enhanced with a Steampunk and Victorian vibe.
- Chef Andrew Ruiz (Bacchus) uses locally sourced meats, cheeses, and house-made ingredients to craft a pub menu with unique flavors.
- Featured items include Wisconsin cheeses, braised bone marrow with crispy sweetbread, and classic fish & chips.

Ryan Braun's Graffito

Modern Italian   www.ryanbraunsgraffito.com
102 North Water Street   @RBGraffito
Milwaukee, WI 53202
414.727.2888

- Deriving its name from the Italian word for "scratch," Ryan Braun's Graffito lives up to the name, as chef Dominic Zumpano (Different Pointe of View, Umami Moto) cooks from scratch, making his own housemade pastas, breads, mozzarella, and sauces.
- Zumpano follows his family's culinary traditions, to create an Italian inspired small plates menu with a great Italian sensibility.
- Using fresh local product, Zumpano's menus includes dishes like scallop small plate, osso buco, and Kobe skirt steak.
- Indeed, Milwaukee Brewers superstar Ryan Braun is a co-owner.

For a complete list of Milwaukee food resources, visit kundaeats.com/milwaukee.

The Bachelor Farmer

Nordic   www.thebachelorfarmer.com
50 North 2nd Avenue   @bachelorfarmer
Minneapolis, MN 55401
612.206.3920

- Minnesota scions Eric and Andrew Dayton (sons of Minnesota's governor, grandsons of the Target stores founder) partner with chef Paul Berglund (Oliveto) in this ambitious Nordic food project.
- The Bachelor Farmer was named 2011 Minneapolis restaurant of the year by the *Star Tribune*.
- Located in a historic North Loop warehouse, the restaurant shares its space with the basement speakeasy Marvel Bar (separate back entrance).

Heidi's

New American   www.heidismpls.com
2903 Lyndale Avenue South   @HeidisMpls
Minneapolis, MN 55408   shefzilla.com (food blog)
612.354.3512

- Rebuilt after a devastating fire, chef Stewart Woodman's (Five Restaurant and Street Lounge) second iteration of Heidi's soared like a phoenix rising from the ashes.
- The Lyn-Lake restaurant prides itself in providing "four-star dining experiences at two-star prices."
- The menu changes frequently with the seasons, but diners can't go wrong with ordering fish dishes from the Le Bernardin alum. Both a 9 and 13 courses Chef's Table menu are also available for the adventurous.

Pizzeria Lola

Wood-Oven Pizza
5557 Xerxes Avenue South
Minneapolis, MN 55410
612.424.8338

www.pizzerialola.com
@PizzeriaLola

- South Minneapolitans are being wowed by the pizza creations coming out of Pizzeria Lola's Le Panyol wood-oven.
- (From owner Ann Kim) "A Korean immigrant, inspired by the pure love of food, joy and her mother's own delicious cooking, quits her day job, opens an artisan pizza pie place and names it after her dog. There's no need to be overly patriotic here, but is there anything more American than that?"
- Yeah, that pretty much sums it up.

Sun Street Breads

Bakery
4600 Nicollet Avenue
Minneapolis, MN 55419
612.354.3414

www.sunstreetbreads.com
@sunstreetbreads

- It's not often a bakery makes a "best restaurant" list, but master baker Solveig Tofte's (Turtle Bread Company) temple of flour in Kingfield is more than worthy.
- Tofte is a competitive baker having represented the USA at the Coupe du Monde de la Boulangerie in Paris.
- Sun Street's open-source menu lists every single ingredient of every single item along with professorial baking notes. Made-from-scratch artisan baguettes (flour, water, salt, yeast, and malt powder) serve as the foundation for delicious delicatessen-style sandwiches.

Tilia

American Brasserie   www.tiliampls.com
2726 West 43rd Street   @tiliampls
Minneapolis, MN 55410
612.354.2806

- One of the Twin Cities' most celebrated chefs, Steven Brown (Café Levain), finally becomes a restaurant owner with Tilia.
- The no-reservations neighborhood "Brasserie Americana" offers "familiar dishes and flavors in new contexts" (e.g., potted meat as duck rillette) at wallet-friendly prices. Lines ensue.
- The word Tilia is the Latin genus for the Linden tree from which the neighborhood Linden Hills derives its name.

Travail Kitchen and Amusements

Gastropub   www.travailkitchen.com
4154 West Broadway Avenue   @Travailkitchen
Robbinsdale, MN 55422
763.535.1131

- Chefs James Winberg and Mike Brown's (Porter & Frye) experimental gastropub shows off the latest molecular gastronomy techniques in a most unlikely suburban strip mall location.
- At $80 for two (time of publishing), Travail's 10-course tasting menu where cooks double as servers could be the best "bang for your buck" meal in America. Alinea at McDonald's prices.
- A no reservations policy further adds to the prole vibe.

For a complete list of Minneapolis food resources, visit kundaeats.com/minneapolis.

The Catbird Seat

New American
1711 Division Street
Nashville, TN 37203
615.248.8458

www.thecatbirdseatrestaurant.com
@SHprojects

- An exciting new collaboration between chefs Josh Habiger (Fat Duck, CRAFT, Alinea) and Erik Anderson (French Laundry, Noma), The Catbird Seat aims to reinvent fine dining in Nashville.
- The "menu" is constantly evolving and no two evenings will be the same. It is largely based on what is fresh, both in terms of ingredients and inspiration for the chefs.
- 32 seats surround an open U-shaped kitchen where you can watch and interact with the chefs as they prepare each dish.

Kayne Prime

Steakhouse
1103 McGavock Street
Nashville, TN 37203
615.259.0050

www.mstreetnashville.com
@KaynePrime

- M Street Development's latest restaurant in the trendy Gulch neighborhood, Kayne Prime, joins their other ventures in the area, Tavern, Whiskey Kitchen, and Virago, as the crown jewel.
- Chef Robbie Wilson offers modern interpretations of the classics, as well as market-driven fresh, farm-to-table creations.
- With nothing less than the best USDA Prime beef, try the Progression of New York Sirloin. For the non-beef eaters, pacific halibut, and lobster mac and cheese will do nicely.

NY Pie

New York Style Pizza   www.realnypie.com
6800 Charlotte Pike, Suite 105
Nashville, TN 37209
615.915.1617

- New York Style pizza comes to Nashville, by way of New Jersey, thanks to owner Greg Meyer.
- Meyer grew up in New Jersey and learned the "tricks of the trade" in making fresh dough and sauce.
- All of the essential elements of a great pizza joint are represented here: dough prepared fresh daily, sauce made fresh from imported Italian tomatoes, and a brick oven.
- New York transplants have said the pizza here is reminiscent to what you'll find in New York's West Village.

For a complete list of Nashville food resources, visit kundaeats.com/nashville.

Cowbell

American   www.cowbell-nola.com
1200 Eagle Street   @cowbellnola
New Orleans, LA 70118
504.298.8689

- Everything at Cowbell begins with their natural grass-fed beef hamburger on potato roll and agogo sauce. Diners can upgrade their burgers with tasty add-ons like apple wood smoked bacon and onion compote.
- Vegetarians are not left out as there is a homemade brown rice and red bean harvest veggie version of the signature burger.
- Chef Brack May (Cobalt), who played collegiate volleyball, comes from an avid sports family. His sister is two-time Olympic gold medalist Misty May-Treanor.

Dominique's on Magazine

French   www.dominiquesonmag.com
4213 Magazine Street
New Orleans, LA 70115
504.261.8253

- Born on the island of Mauritius in the Indian Ocean, chef Dominique Macquet grew up with Creole, Asian, African and Indian home-cooked dishes, and combines that tropical influence with French technique.
- Macquet has traveled the world, cooking at the White House and the U.S. Embassy in Paris, but his favorite memory is cooking Nelson Mandela's first meal outside South African prison walls.
- The new Dominique's will be opening in Mid-2012.

Rue 127

New American   www.rue127.com
127 North Carrollton Avenue
New Orleans, LA 70119
504.483.1571

- Chef Ray Gruezke (Commander's Palace, Le Foret), a true New Orleans native, opens his first restaurant in the heart of historic Mid-City, placing it in a renovated 19th Century New Orleans style shotgun home.
- Gruezke uses local, sustainable produce whenever possible, and the menu changes weekly to highlight the freshest products. Roast chicken and pan-seared puppy drum are among the many wonderful, artfully prepared dishes.
- Be sure to save room for one of pastry chef Joanna Palmer's desserts, especially, the napoleon of Creole cream cheese.

Sylvain

Gastropub   www.sylvainnola.com
625 Chartres Street   @sylvainnola
New Orleans, LA 70130
504.265.8123

- Former Men's Journal editor Sean McCusker and Robert Leblanc (Loa, Capdeville) collaborate on this French Quarter gastropub.
- The menu offers a number of "elevated bistro" choices including buttermilk-fried chicken sandwiches and Veuve Clicquot champagne with fries ($50).
- Sylvain sits inside a historic carriage house that once housed a notorious brothel owned by Madame Rose Arnold. The restaurant honors "Aunt Rose" every night with an offering of Sazerac to her spirit.

Three Muses

Gastropub
536 Frenchmen Street
New Orleans, LA 70116
504.298.8746

www.thethreemuses.com
@threemusesnola

- This restaurant/music club/bar, located on Frenchmen Street, is owned by three co-muses, who each bring a unique skill set to the table: Christopher Starnes (restaurateur), Sophie Lee (musician), and Daniel Esses (chef).
- Chef Esses (Café Degas, Marigny Brasserie) changes the globally-inspired small plates menu frequently with dishes like duck pastrami pizza and Korean boolgogi rice bowl.
- For cocktails, try the house Muse (fresh cucumbers and strawberries with St Germain & Plymouth Gin).

For a complete list of New Orleans food resources, visit kundaeats.com/neworleans.

Ai Fiori

Ligurian   www.aifiorinyc.com
400 5th Avenue   @aifiori
New York, NY 10018
212.613.8660

- Ai Fiori means "among the flowers."
- Inside the swanky Setai Fifth Avenue Hotel, Italian-trained chef Michael White (Marea, Alto) explores the food of the Ligurian Sea.
- French and Italian seafood dishes dominate the menu with signature dishes like mare e monte (diver scallops, celery root, burgundy black truffles, bone marrow, thyme), astice (scotia lobster, root vegetable fondant, château chalon), and fresh sardines.

Boulud Sud

Mediterranean   www.danielnyc.com
20 West 64th Street   @BouludSud
New York, NY 10023
212.595.1313

- Legendary French chef Daniel Boulud does Mediterranean!
- The menu is structured in three sections: "De La Mer" (Sea), "Du Jardin" (Garden), and "De La Ferme" (Farm). Signature dishes include crispy vegetables (seasonal), harira, sardine escabèche, loup de mer, and Tuscan rib-eye.
- Pastry chef Ghaya Oliveira's grapefruit givré was all the rage among the New York City critics.
- The Upper West Side location is open and bright (slate and sunflower) featuring a communal polygonal bar for tapas.

Brushstroke

Japanese   www.davidbouley.com
30 Hudson Street
New York, NY 10013
212.791.3771

- In collaboration with Yoshki Tusji's Cooking Academy, French legend David Bouley (Bouley Restaurant) imports the clean tastes of Japanese kaiseki cuisine to his Tribeca empire.
- Chef Isao Yamada's menu is meticulously organized by eight or ten tasting courses climaxing with a classic seafood rice duet. Per tradition, simple plates made of lacquered wood act as a canvas giving the food a certain artistic element.
- Japan's Super Potato designed the minimalist Kyoto cool interior calling attention to the massive open kitchen.

Cannibal

Belgian   www.thecannibalnyc.com
113 East 29th Street   @CannibalNYC
New York, NY 10016
212.686.5480

- (Human-free) meat and beer. The name of this eclectic café-retail hybrid is actually an homage to dominant '70s Belgian cyclist Eddy Merckx. Diners can peruse and buy bicycle parts whilst sampling various cured meats.
- Chef-butcher Christian Pappanicholas' (Resto) passion for charcuterie and whole animal butchery is evident with a Belgian-inspired menu that lists everything from lamb tartare to slow roasted pig's head. An aged steak du jour is available for the less adventurous.
- A communal bar presents over 450 international beer choices with seven rotating drafts.

Danji

Korean   www.danjinyc.com
346 West 52 Street   @danjinyc
New York, New York 10019
212.586.2880

- Leading the midtown Manhattan Korean new wave, chef Hooni Kim (Daniel, Masa) applies modern technique to traditional Hanguk dishes.
- Danji's small plates menu splits into two distinct sections: Traditional ("spicy old-school stinky" shigol dwenjang jjigae, japchae) and Modern (kimchi bacon chorizo paella, bulgogi beef sliders).
- The small, minimalist space holds surprises, including hidden table drawers housing the menu.

The Dutch

American   www.thedutchnyc.com
131 Sullivan Street
New York, NY 10012
212.677.6200

- "Just an American joint that serves nice food, wine and spirits." The Dutch was probably the hottest SoHo restaurant in 2011; ergo, the hottest restaurant in New York (and hence the world).
- Chef Andrew Carmellini (Locanda Verde, A Voce) offers an interesting selection of Yankee melting pot comfort foods (steaks for two, fried chicken with honey butter biscuit, pie).
- The oyster bar choices range from the wildly popular $5 little oyster sandwich to the massive $135 Prince Platter (oysters, little necks, bay scallops, kampachi, sweet shrimp, uni, lobster cocktail, crab claws).

Empellon

Mexican-Tacos
230 West 4th Street
New York, NY 10014
212.367.0999

www.empellon.com
@empellon

- While chef Alex Stupak (Clio, Alinea, wd~50) may have gotten his start in fine dining, his move to more casual, simple fare with Empellon benefits us all.
- Stupak opened the restaurant with the intention of treating tacos with a high level of respect and serving them in a fun environment. Thankfully, he has succeeded.
- Inventive tacos, such as lamb barbacoa with salsa borracha, beer braised tongue with potatoes and arbol chile salsa, and lobster with field corn and epazote, will challenge your perception about this Mexican staple.

Isa

New American
348 Wythe Avenue
Brooklyn, NY 11211
347.689.3594

www.isa.gg
@Isanyc

- Williamsburg art experiment or restaurant? Probably a little of both.
- In owner-designer Taavo Somer's (Freemans and Peels) own words, Isa is a "primitive, modern house of fun with firewood."
- That firewood fuels the wood-oven based food, everything from fresh breads to smoked fish to seared vegetables.
- Chef Ignacio Mattos (Argentine) updates his dadaist menu frequently walking the line of rustic and intergalactic.

La Mar Cebicheria Peruana

Peruvian
11 Madison Avenue
New York, NY 10010
212.612.3388

www.lamarcebicheria.com
@lamar_nyc

- Gastón Acurio (Astrid & Gastón), Lima's most famous chef, exports the latest outpost of his La Mar Cebichería Peruana franchise to Manhattan.
- "Cebichería" cuisine is staged prominently using sashimi grade seafood (fluke, hamachi, yellowfin) and the derivative leche de tigre (key lime juice, hot peppers, spices, fish shrapnel).
- The rest of the menu features a wide selection of heritage dishes (anticuchos, causas, lomo saltado).
- Lost in translation? La Mar's website blogs a helpful Peruvian gastronomy encyclopedia.

La Promenade Des Anglais

French-Italian
461 West 23rd Street
New York, NY 10011
212.255.7400

www.lapromenadenyc.com
@lapromenadenyc

- Tucked inside Chelsea's London Terrace Towers alongside The High Line, chef-owner Alain Allegretti (Atelier, Le Cirque 2000) channels his childhood by exploring coastal French cooking.
- Cote D'Azur style fish dishes are clearly the focus (the cod headliner is mixed with Perugina sausage, potatoes, and olives), but don't overlook the Italian pasta dishes.
- Named after a street in Nice, the classy space evokes the Riviera town with its checkerboard marble floors, brass lighting, blue velour benches, and beach murals.

M. Wells (closed)
French-Canadian   www.mwellsdiner.com
2117 49th Avenue
Long Island City, NY 11101

- Hardly Knew Ye. Before its abrupt closure stemming from a lease dispute, M. ("Magasin," French for "store") Wells was probably the most talked about new restaurant in America. The media impressions included everything from a No Reservations segment to an ugly tiff with GQ's chief food critic Alan Richman.
- From this unlikely Long Island City location, husband and wife owners, Hugue Dufour (Au Pied de Cochon) and Sarah Obraitis, stunned diners and critics alike with their "Quebeco-American" mash-ups.
- Rumor has it a new location is currently being scouted.

RedFarm
Chinese   www.redfarmnyc.com
529 Hudson Street   @redfarmnyc
New York, NY 10014
212.792.9700

- Chef Joe Ng (Chinatown Brasserie) and Ed Schoenfeld join forces to create this West Village "greenmarket" Chinese restaurant.
- Ng, the dumpling whisperer, experiments with crazy dim sum filling combinations (Exhibit A: Katz's Pastrami with hot ballpark mustard). He is clearly having fun with the shrimp-filled "Pacman dumpling."
- Asian big plate options include nouvelle rice hot pots and elevated noodle bowls.

Red Rooster

Soul Food   www.redroosterharlem.com
310 Malcolm X Boulevard   @roosterharlem
Harlem, NY 10027
212.792.9001

- Red Rooster is inspired by the legendary 20th century speakeasy of the same name, a popular hang-out for many of Harlem's top artists and intellectuals.
- Swedish-born chef, Marcus Samuelsson (Aquavit), creates global soul food using high-end ingredients and Top Chef Master technique. Popular picks include improvised versions of dirty rice, fried chicken, and oxtails.
- The restaurant is every bit as much a community project (Samuelson lives there) as it is a dining destination, by hiring local neighborhood kids and teaching cooking classes.

Salinas

Spanish   www.salinasnyc.com
136 9th Avenue   @salinasnyc
New York, NY 10011
212.776.1990

- Named after Balearic Island salt farms, Salinas brings Spanish coast tapas cuisine to Chelsea.
- Chef Luis Bollo (Mediterra, Meigas) deftly crafts big and small plates inspired by his home country, including Ibérico ham, langostinos al ajillo, gazpacho de primavera, and paella negra (cuttlefish-ink blackened Calasparra rice, monk fish, clams, mussels, green beans and lemon zest aioli).
- Fruit-infused sangria is the centerpiece drink, while over 75 Spanish wines are available. Drink under the stars by the fireplace inside their retractable glass roof area.

Shelsky's Smoked Fish

Jewish   www.shelskys.com
251 Smith Street   @Shelskys
Brooklyn, NY 11231
718.855.8817

- Shelsky's harks back to the golden age of the old New York Eastern European delis and appetizing stores.
- The Carroll Gardens restaurant is a veritable shul of smoked fish (pickled herring, gravlax, sable, whitefish), and owner Peter Shelsky is the rabbi.
- Homemade sandwiches and salads round up the menu, with bagels and bialys sourced from Kossar's (Davidivich on the Sabbath).
- Sweets like babka, rugelach, and honey cake are all baked in-house and from scratch.

St. Anselm

American Wood Grill
355 Metropolitan Avenue
Brooklyn, NY 11211
718.384.5054

- Owner Joe Carroll (Fette Sau, Spuyten Duyvil) pivots Williamsburg's St. Anselm from hipster fried bar food to (value-priced) carnivore wood grill.
- Start your journey with an "Iceberg & Blue" (iceberg lettuce, bacon and blue cheese dressing) before advancing to one of chef Yvon de Tassigny's many meat and seafood dishes.
- The giant axe handle rib eye is value priced by the ounce.
- The sweet (tea) brined young chicken gained notoriety for leaving the head and feet in the presentation.

Tertulia

Spanish-Tapas
359 Sixth Avenue
New York, NY 10014
646.559.9909

www.tertulianyc.com
@tertulianyc

- Naming his restaurant after a type of Spanish literary salon popular in the 17th century, chef Seamus Mullen (Boqueria) brings together the spirit of the tertulia with a menu that celebrates Spain's exquisite products and flavors.
- Mullen focuses on the simple, rustic cuisine of the Asturias region of Spain, which is famous for its cheeses, seafood, beef and beans.
- Items such as croquetas de jamon iberico, rabo de toro, and cojonudo... revisited, fill out the creative menu.

For a complete list of New York food resources, visit kundaeats.com/nyc.

Dolce Cafe

American Bistro   www.dolcecafeomaha.com
12317 West Maple Road   @DolceOmaha
Omaha, NE 68164
402.964.2212

- Service is paramount at chef-owner Gina Stern's new restaurant. Each customer is made to feel important at Dolce Cafe, so don't be surprised if Stern greets you at your table and chats you up, describing your dish to you in detail.
- Stern is devoted to creating a healthy menu, and to that end, she sources organics wherever she can on a weekly basis.
- Working with local farmers, Stern offers healthy items like fresh Atlantic salmon, grass fed beef, and all natural chicken.

The Grey Plume

New American Farm-to-Table   www.thegreyplume.com
220 South 31st Avenue, Suite 3101   @TheGreyPlume
Omaha, NE 68131
402.763.4447

- Along with excellent cuisine, environmental consciousness is at the forefront of chef-owner Clayton Chapman's (Tru Restaurant, V. Mertz) new restaurant.
- The Grey Plume is the first 4-Star Sustainabuild™ Certified Green Restaurant from the Green Restaurant Association, making it the nation's greenest and most sustainable restaurant. Many items in the restaurant are recycled.
- Chapman employs a true farm-to-table approach, offering a seasonally driven menu that places great emphasis on locally grown produce and livestock. The menu changes continuously based on the freshest items available.

Saigon Surface

French-Vietnamese   www.saigonsurface.com
324 South 14th Street   @SaigonSurface
Omaha, NE 68102
402.614.4496

- Saigon Surface will challenge any preconceptions you may have about Vietnamese restaurants, as Vietnam goes decidedly high tech at owner Tu Nguyen's newest venture.
- Complementing the sleek décor, iPads are located at every table and can be used to order your food, and then check e-mails and listen to music, creating an entertaining atmosphere.
- Chef Be Lam's modern take on French Vietnamese cuisine yields popular, authentic dishes such as oxtail pho, 18-Hour boneless short ribs, signature grilled pork, and pineapple fried rice.

For a complete list of Omaha food resources, visit kundaeats.com/omaha.

Hawkers Asian Street Fare

Asian Fusion-Tapas   www.facebook.com/hawkersstreetfare
1103 North Mills Avenue   @hawkersfare
Orlando, FL 32803
407.237.0606

- Hawkers Asian Street Fare is named after the popular outdoor food stall markets in Asia where "hawkers" shout out their daily offerings to passersby.
- The Asian street market comes to Orlando, offering authentic Asian street food with a small plate approach.
- Blending various Asian cuisines, including Korean, Malaysian, Chinese, Indian, and Vietnamese, the menu is diverse and satisfying, with most dishes costing $6 or less.
- Authentic dishes include roast duck udon noodle soup, five spice fish tacos, and roti canai.

Tibby's New Orleans Kitchen

Cajun   www.tibbysneworleanskitchen.com
2203 Aloma Avenue
Winter Park, FL 32792
407.672.5753

- The Big Easy comes to Orlando, courtesy of owner Brian Wheeler (Tijuana Flats). The restaurant is named after his late uncle, Walter Tabony, a lifelong New Orleans native.
- You'll find all the classics of New Orleans style Cajun cuisine here, including shrimp and andouille cheddar grits, chicken and sausage gumbo, shrimp creole, and catfish po-boys.
- The décor is casual, while being vibrant, with New Orleans artwork on the wall, and jazz playing from the speakers.

For a complete list of Orlando food resources, visit kundaeats.com/orlando.

Barbuzzo

Mediterranean   www.barbuzzo.com
110 South 13th Street   @barbuzzo
Philadelphia, PA 19107
215.546.9300

- The chef-developer-empresses of 13th Street, Marcie Turney and Valerie Safran (Lolita, Bindi), set their sights on the Mediterranean.
- Barbuzzo specializes in artisan San Marzano sauced pizzas adding both traditional and new American ingredients.
- To close your meal, be sure to try their famous sea salted vanilla bean caramel budino dessert covered in dark chocolate.

The Farm and Fisherman

New American   www.thefarmandfisherman.com
1120 Pine Street   @FarmFisherman
Philadelphia, PA 19107
267.687.1555

- This small 30 seat BYO restaurant has become one of the most coveted seats in the city.
- Schooled at Blue Hill, the national temple of farm-to-table, rising chef Joshua Lawler (Telepan) brings the "Stone Barns" philosophy to Philly's Washington Square West neighborhood.
- True to its namesake, local, sustainable ingredients lay the foundation of Lawler's daily changing menu. No corporate food trucks park in the alley as all supplies come directly from farms, foragers, or fishermen.

Mica

New American   www.micarestaurant.com
8609 Germantown Avenue
Philadelphia, PA 19118
267.335.3912

- Chef-owner Chip Roman's (Blackfish, Le Bec-Fin) multicourse chalkboard tasting menus wowed the national and Philadelphia food press garnering multiple awards and accolades.
- "Best ingredient" seafood dishes are a particular specialty of the house. Sample dishes include Carolina Spanish Mackerel with radish saboyan foam and Loch Duart Salmon with cauliflower.
- Mica is named after the rock crystals that make up the stone walls of the Chestnut Hill building.

Talula's Garden

New American   www.talulasgarden.com
210 West Washington Square
Philadelphia, PA 19106
215.592.7787

- Talula's Garden is a super collaboration of two Philadelphia restaurant giants: Aimee Olexy (Django, Talula's Table) and Stephen Starr (Buddakan, Morimoto).
- The center cheese bar is the star of the show as local and international cheeses are meticulously curated by the "Maître Fromager" owner.
- Cali-trained chef Sean McPaul (Jardinière, Bacar) has drawn rave reviews for his farmers market dictated, "Hyper-Seasonal" menu.

Tashan

Indian   www.mytashan.com
777 South Broad Street
Philadelphia, PA 19147
267.687.2170

- Restaurateur Munish Narula (Tiffin) continues to challenge the Philadelphian pre-conceptions of Indian food with this Beard nominated upscale fusion grill.
- Executive chef Sylva Senat (Buddakan, Aquavit) composes the dishes with an eye towards creative interpretations of classic Indian fare.
- GQ magazine named Tashan's Naga Beef Sümi (wagyu beef, naga-soy, onion pakora, cucumber-peanut relish) as one of the five best American dishes of the year.

For a complete list of Philadelphia food resources, visit kundaeats.com/philadelphia.

82

Amaro Pizzeria and Vino Lounge

Italian
28234 North Tatum Boulevard
Cave Creek, AZ 85331
480.502.1920

www.amaroaz.com
@AmaroPizzeriaAZ

- Drawing inspiration from his grandfather, owner Frank Vairo (Kazmierez World Wine Bar, The Estate House), brings a taste of Calabrese to Cave Creek with this enoteca pizzeria.
- Wood-fired pizzas are the star of the show featuring fresh mozzarella, private label olive oil, and an array of customized toppings.
- Co-owner Tagan Dering is one of two Cowboy Ciao alumni to make the Kunda Eat's Best New Restaurant 2012 List.

Citizen Public House

Gastropub
7111 East 5th Avenue
Scottsdale, AZ 85251
480.398.4208

www.citizenpublichouse.com
@citizenpubhouse

- Citizen Public House brings the upscale gastropub concept to Old Town Scottsdale.
- Chef Bernie Kantak (Cowboy Ciao) is clearly having fun in the kitchen with playful menu items like "Boof! (there it is) Barramundi" and "Smart chicken is cool! (sweet corn risotto, smoked onion & shitake mushroom hash & truffle oil)" And, yes, the original chopped salad has its own Facebook page: facebook.com/TheOriginalChoppedSalad.
- To pair with the clever food, mixologist Richie Moe has curated an extensive craft beer and cocktail program.

Sekong By Night

Cambodian
1312 East Indian School Road
Phoenix, AZ 8501
480.238.0238

www.sekongbynight.com
@sekongbynight

- The debut of Phoenix's only Cambodian restaurant pleased ex-pats and curious diners alike with authentic Khmer flavors.
- The menu showcases everything from Katheaw soups (rice noodles in chicken broth) to Khmer baguette sandwiches (grilled meats with pate spread).
- The restaurant's name comes from owner Lakhana In's favorite song from the sixties. "Reathrey Sekong" tells the tale of a beautiful girl awaiting her lover on the banks of the Sekong River.

ShinBay

Japanese-Sushi
7001 North Scottsdale Road
Scottsdale, AZ 85253
480.664.0180

www.shinbay.com
@ShinBayJapanese

- ShinBay has quickly emerged as one of metropolitan Phoenix's best sushi options from both a sourcing and technique POV.
- The restaurant could be classified as "New Japanese," as Chef Shinji Kurita weaves modern ingredients and technique into traditional Japanese fare (nigiri, tempura, ceramic hot pot).
- Located in a quiet Scottsdale Seville location, the 30 seat restaurant also features a special omakase dinner available only by reservation.

Tryst Café

International   www.trystcafeaz.com
21050 North Tatum Boulevard   @trystcafe
Phoenix, AZ 85050
480.585.7978

- Serving breakfast, lunch and dinner, Tryst Café offers a healthy locally sourced menu using natural and organic ingredients.
- International influences pepper the menu with dishes like Beef Wellington, Hungarian cornish hen, and Jamaican tilapia.
- With certification from the Gluten Intolerance Group, the restaurant prides itself on a wide variety of wheat protein free choices (and menu modifications).

For a complete list of Phoenix food resources, visit kundaeats.com/phoenix.

Salt of the Earth

New American   www.saltpgh.com
5523 Penn Avenue   @saltpgh
Pittsburgh, PA 15206
412.441.7258

- A collaboration between chef-owner Kevin Sousa (Bigelow Grille) and architects and co-owners Doug and Liza Cruze, the restaurant provides fine dining in a casual atmosphere.
- Using inspiration from around the globe, Sousa uses local ingredients to create dishes such as beef tartare with marrow and quail egg, octopus with chorizo, and hanger steak with broccoli kimchi and wild rice porridge.
- Grab a seat at one of the coveted counter seats that face the open stainless steel kitchen, where you can see Sousa and his team prepare and create these unique dishes.

Spoon

New American Farm-to-Table   www.spoonpgh.com
134 South Highland Avenue   @Spoonpgh
Pittsburgh, PA 15206
412.362.6001

- Executive chef Brian Pekarcik (Steelhead Brasserie) creates a farm-to-table menu that focuses on using products that are fresh, local, and sustainable from the Pittsburgh area.
- The menu is seasonal and changes accordingly to ensure that only the freshest and most local ingredients are used.
- Pekarcik uses a variety of global influences, as evidenced by items like pork belly "banh mi," tandoori salmon, gorgonzola blue cheese soufflé, and lamb and gnocchi.

For a complete list of Pittsburgh food resources, visit kundaeats.com/pittsburgh.

Petite Jacqueline

French   www.bistropj.com
190 State Street   @BistroPJ
Portland, ME 04101
207.553.7044

- Michelle Corry and Liz Koenigsberg (Five Fifty-Five Restaurant) garnered national recognition (Beard Award) for their affordable riff on the traditional French bistro.
- Located in Portland's West End Arts District, the menu draws inspiration from Corry's French grandmother, the namesake Jacqueline.
- Classic dishes like soupe à l'oignon, quiche du jour, and foie gras round up the menu.

For a complete list of Portland food resources, visit kundaeats.com/portlandme.

87

Little Bird

French Bistro   www.littlebirdbistro.com
219 Southwest 6th Avenue   @lbbistro
Portland, OR 97205
503.688.5952

- Little Bird is the second restaurant from wunderkind chef, Gabriel Rucker (Le Pigeon), who won the James Beard Rising Star Chef Award for the best chef aged 30 or younger in 2011.
- Rucker won universal acclaim for his first restaurant, Le Pigeon, and decided to take that concept and make it more diner friendly and accessible with Little Bird.
- Chef Erik Van Kley doesn't disappoint by offering traditional items like duck confit, the Le Pigeon burger, and what has been called the best ham-and-cheese sandwich in Portland.

Natural Selection

Vegetarian-Vegan   www.naturalselectionpdx.com
3033 Northeast Alberta Street
Portland, OR 97211
503.288.5883

- Vegetarians and vegans in Portland have plenty of reason to celebrate as chef Aaron Woo (La Folie, The Cosmopolitan Restaurant, Clarklewis) brings high end cuisine to the plant based world.
- Woo's menu is built on vegetables, fruits, and grains, and combines both rustic and modern cooking techniques while highlighting the flavors of France, Italy, and Spain.
- Two four-course menus are offered, one vegetarian and the other vegan, and much of it is gluten free. The menu changes weekly, and focuses on seasonal and local food.

St. Jack

French Bistro
2039 Southeast Clinton Street
Portland, OR 97202
503.360.1281

www.stjackpdx.com
@stjackpdx

- Chef Aaron Barnett (Gary Danko, 23 Hoyt) pays homage to the bouchons, or esteemed cafes of Lyon, France, by providing his take on rustic French cuisine.
- Featuring both a traditional pâtisserie and restaurant, St. Jacks is ensconced in a quaint 19th century home.
- Barnett focuses on traditional Lyonnais dishes done well, and items such as fried tripe, blood pudding, frog legs, coq à la bière, and pieds de cochon are indicative of his passion for the cuisine.

For a complete list of Portland food resources, visit kundaeats.com/portland.

Gregoria's Kitchen and Cuban Steakhouse

Steak House-Cuban   www.gregoriaskitchen.com
2818 Chapel Hill Road   @GregoriasDurham
Durham, NC 27707
919.797.2747

- Chef Dania Gonzalez (Café Giorgios, George's Garage) channels her Cuban mom's recipes with a diverse menu featuring Havana meat dishes paired with fried plantains (your choice of either green tostones or sweet maduros).
- Located inside a nostalgic Durham property (previously, the fifty year old Peddler Steakhouse), the restaurant honors the location by offering a number of steak options with the signature dish being ropa vieja (shredded garlic skirt steak with tomatoes).
- Cuba's national drink, the mojito, is a popular choice.

MacchuPicchu

Peruvian   www.machupicchuperuviancuisine.com
4500 Falls of Neuse Road #100
Raleigh, NC 27609
919.526.7378

- The Peruvian cuisine wave of 2011 hit the triangle area with the opening of MachuPicchu in North Raleigh.
- Chef Gloria Orhuela's (Johnson & Wales Apprenti Cuisinier Award winner) "Nouveau Andean" menu features modern takes on the foundational classics of Peru: ceviche in leche de tigre, jalea, lomo saltado, fried yucca, and more. Sadly, no guinea pig on a stick.
- For dessert, try the unique Mazamorra Morada (purple corn and fruit pudding).

Mandolin

New American-Southern   www.mandolinraleigh.com
2519 Fairview Road   @MandolinNC
Raleigh, NC 27608
919.322.0365

- Straight out of a storybook, hometown boy Sean Fowler (Fearrington House) returns to Raleigh, opening his first restaurant in a restored pharmacy from his childhood.
- Mandolin serves approachable Southern food with global influences using local ingredients from the North Carolina coast and farmlands.
- One of the menu favorites is usually some riff on fried chicken (with pimento cheese or buckwheat-buttermilk waffles).
- Charles Kirkwood's cocktail program rotates weekly.

Vimala's Curryblossom Café

Indian   www.curryblossom.com
431 West Franklin Street   @Curryblossom
Chapel Hill, NC 27516
919.929.3833

- Vimala's farm-to-fork, social justice approach (living wages and sustainable practices) has garnered the restaurant a cult following in progressive Chapel Hill.
- Owner Vimala Rajendran regularly hosts community supported dinners and has instituted an "everybody eats" policy whereby menu prices can slide based on need.
- In addition to local farm suppliers, the restaurant utilizes ingredients from a kitchen garden to craft a wide array of Mumbai-inspired dishes.

For a complete list of Raleigh food resources, visit kundaeats.com/raleigh.

The Roosevelt

Southern
623 North 25th Street
Richmond, VA 23223
804.658.1935

www.rooseveltrva.com
@rooseveltrva

- The Roosevelt is a "New Southern" collaboration between chefs Kendra Feather (Garnett's, Ipanema) and Lee Gregory (Mockingbird, Six Burner).
- Signature dishes include crispy pig head terrine, southern poutine, pork cheeks with cheese grits, and Coca-Cola cake.
- To pair with the heavily locally sourced menu, the wine list is exclusively made up of Virginia labels.
- Located in the historic Church Hill district of Richmond, the 19th century building oozes ambiance with its tin ceiling and antique church pew seats.

Stella's

Greek
1012 Lafayette Street
Richmond, VA 23221
804.358.2011

www.stellasrichmond.com
@stellasrichmond

- Third time's the charm. Stella Dikos, the grand dame of the Richmond dining world, hits every mark with her latest namesake restaurant.
- Classic Hellenic and Greek-American dishes with Herculean sized portions are the standards.
- Revel in libation from the all-Greek wine list whilst classic Greek films project silently on the western wall.

For a complete list of Richmond food resources, visit kundaeats.com/richmond.

The Press Bistro

Mediterranean Bistro   www.thepressbistro.com
1809 Capitol Avenue   @ThePressBistro
Sacramento, CA 95811
916.444.2566

- Chef-owner David English's (Ella) draws inspirations from French bistros and Italian trattorias to form the base for his latest restaurant.
- The menu offers numerous inviting tapas and appetizers, such as fried meatballs with garlic-yogurt sauce, potato croquettes, crisp pork belly and grilled octopus. Signature entrees include hanger steak, grilled ono, and wild salmon.
- A selection of wines from Spain, France, and Italy complement the menu.

Sergio's Steak & Seafood

Italian   www.sergiosfolsom.com
322 East Bidwell Street   @sergiosfolsom
Folsom, CA 95630
916.983.4300

- Owned by Sergio and Francesca Mirabelli, Sergio's is an Italian steak and seafood restaurant known for their authentic cuisine and hearty portions.
- Chef Antonio Principato, originally from Sicily, has peppered the menu with unique offerings of wild game, such as boar, osso buco, buffalo, and game birds.
- Traditional Italian offerings are ever present, with pollo alla piccata, veal parmigianna, and lasagna ferrarese.

For a complete list of Sacramento food resources, visit kundaeats.com/sacramento.

Bogart's Smokehouse

BBQ   www.bogartssmokehouse.com
1627 South 9th Street
Saint Louis, MO 63104
314.621.3107

- It takes a bit of brashness to open a new barbeque restaurant in the hypercompetitive St. Louis market, but veteran pit master Skip Steele (Supersmokers, Pappy's Smokehouse) was easily up for the challenge.
- The Soulard smokehouse specializes in glazed pork ribs in both full and half racks, but the cow options (brisket, pastrami, prime rib) should not be underestimated.
- The mandatory side of choice is pit baked beans.

Home Wine Kitchen

New American   www.homewinekitchen.com
7322 Manchester Road   @homewinekitchen
Maplewood, MO 63143
314.802.7676

- On "No Menu Monday," chef-owner Cassy Vires (Viking Cooking School) will micro-customize a three course menu based on the answers to a brief questionnaire (allergies/dislikes, favorite foods/what you make at home, thoughts on pork belly).
- For the other days, the new American upscale comfort food menu changes weekly to reflect the seasons and ingredient availability.
- The Maplewood restaurant features a vast palette of value wine all priced at $30/bottle or $8/glass (time of printing).

Riverbend Restaurant & Bar

Creole
701 Utah Street
Saint Louis, MO 63118
314.664.8443

www.riverbendbar.com
@Riverbendbar

- New Orleans native Sam Kogos (Rendon Inn) and his cousin, chef Steve Daney, bring authentic Creole recipes up the Mississippi River to the historic South Soulard area.
- All of the Louisiana classics are available, from shrimp-oyster-catfish gumbo to cochon de lait po-boys to crawfish étouffée.
- For dessert, the decadent Creole bread pudding is house-made, topped with golden raisins and Sazerac whiskey-cream sauce.

Salt

American Larder
4356 Lindell Boulevard
Saint Louis, MO 63108
314.932.5787

www.enjoysalt.com
@enjoysalt

- Located in the Central West End, Salt is chef Wes Johnson's (Eclipse, Shaved Duck) first owned restaurant.
- Subscribing to the proximity cooking philosophy, the restaurant showcases product from nearby Missouri and Illinois farms: "the best meals have traveled the least from farm-to-table."
- The availability of Missouri River Valley waterfowl is evident as the menu boasts a number of duck fat fried options including buttermilk fried chicken and frites. For those who want the whole duck, the "sorghum-lacquered" breast is sweet and savory.

The Tavern Kitchen & Bar

New American   www.tavernstl.com
2961 Dougherty Ferry Road
Saint Louis, MO 63122
636.825.0600

- Mastering his craft in Manhattan and Chicago kitchens, chef Justin Haifley (Roy's, Tru) returns home to St. Louis, specifically, Valley Park, with this "exquisite comfort food" tavern.
- Simple, familiar dishes like meatloaf, ravioli, and mac and cheese are reinvented with modern ingredients and technique.
- Haifley's Bacon and Eggs (pork belly, brioche, one hour sous-vide egg) personified this approach and was all the talk of the St. Louis food press.

For a complete list of St. Louis food resources, visit kundaeats.com/stlouis.

96

Dojo Asian Inspired Cuisine and Lounge
Japanese-Sushi   www.dojoslc.com
423 West 300 South, Ste 150   @dojoslc
Salt Lake City, UT 84101
801.328.3333

- A Dojo is any place that leads to living in the Present, and this is the inspiration that chef-owner Kirk Terashima and his partner Kelly Shiotani used as they envisioned an environment that would help you live in the moment.
- Dojo offers a dining and drinking experience where superlative food, gracious hospitality, and affordable value are of the utmost importance.
- High quality sushi (flown in from San Francisco), ramen noodles, and other Asian entrees fill the menu, but two standouts are the Guchi roll and the White Dragon.

The Farm at Canyons Resort
Locally Sourced New American   www.canyonsresort.com
4900 Canyons Resort Drive
Park City, UT 84098
435.615.8080

- Located in the heart of Canyons Ski Resort, The Farm is a rustic, yet refined restaurant that is a welcome addition to the Park City culinary scene, courtesy of Talisker Corporation.
- Chef John Murcko (Talisker on Main) crafts an innovative menu that focuses on locally sourced ingredients from farms and artisans within 200 miles of Park City.
- The local influence is evident in items like Summit County beef rib-eye, Morgan Valley lamb shank, Mountain Valley rainbow trout, and Heritage bourbon pork rib-eye.

Penny Ann's Café

Homemade Comfort Food   www.pennyannscafe.com
1810 South Main Street
Salt Lake City, UT 84115
801.935.4760

- Penny Ann's Café is a true family operation, with chef-owner Warren Willey (Westgate Grill, Maxwell's East Coast Eatery), his sister, Penny Ann, his parents, and in-laws all involved.
- Penny Ann's serves up fresh homemade dishes in a comfortable cafe setting and was recently voted the best and most affordable breakfast in Salt Lake City.
- Everything on the menu is made in house and you'll notice the quality as you try the grilled Reuben, and Philly cheesesteak.
- All items cost less than $7.99, even the killer desserts.

Sala Thai Kitchen

Thai   www.salathaikitchen.com
679 South 200 West   @SalaThaiKitchen
Salt Lake City, UT 84101
801.328.2499

- Owner-chef Jitrada Dreier has brought the authentic tastes of her home in Phetchabun, in north Thailand, to SLC.
- The restaurant space is spacious and modern while eschewing the normal Thai kitsch found in many other restaurants, instead opting to showcase art and photography from local artists.
- Dreier showcases her dishes in stunning presentations, so dishes like pad him ma parn and pra ram look as good as they taste.

For a complete list of Salt Lake City food resources, visit kundaeats.com/slc.

The Monterey

Gastropub   www.themontereysa.com
1127 South St Mary's Street   @TheMontereySA
San Antonio, TX 78210
210.745.2581

- The Monterey virtually defines what a great gastropub is all about, offering high quality, creative, inexpensive food, and a beer list that celebrates craft brewers and microbreweries.
- Chef Albert Vasquez turns the concept of fine dining on its head by using exotic, fresh, high quality ingredients in a setting that is fun, casual and friendly.
- The adventurous will love exciting dishes like pork belly, squid ragout, beef cheeks, pig's feet, and lamb sandwiches.

Restaurant Gwendolyn

Classic American – Farm-to-Table   www.restaurantgwendolyn.com
152 East Pecan Street, Suite 100   @RestGwendolyn
San Antonio, TX 78205
210.222.1849

- Even in a world of increasing "Farm-to-Table" restaurants, Restaurant Gwendolyn stands out for its authenticity.
- Chef Michael Sohocki (Le Reve, The Cove) employs a true old world philosophy, using only what was available and doing as they did before the Industrial Revolution (1850).
- There are no blenders, mixers, deep fryers, freezers, nor anything else with a motor and nothing with a plug.
- Every perishable ingredient comes from within 150 miles of the restaurant. The menu changes daily and all items are handmade using only fresh, local, and seasonal ingredients.

For a complete list of San Antonio food resources, visit kundaeats.com/sanantonio.

Davanti Enoteca

Italian   www.davantisandiego.com
1655 India Street   @davantisandiego
San Diego, CA 92101
619.237.9606

- Noted Chicago chef and restaurateur Scott Harris (Francesca Group) brings his authentic Italian restaurant concept to Little Italy in San Diego with his latest venture, Davanti Enoteca.
- Chef Luigi Negroni (Donatello) started his career in Imola, Italy and brings that authenticity with him as he prepares simple, rustic dishes that elevate traditional Italian cuisine.
- As expected, traditional fare dominates, with dishes like polpo con rafano, spada Davanti, and the famous Davanti burger with bacon jam, roasted tomato and cheese curd.

Eddie V's Prime Seafood

Steak Seafood   www.eddievsrestaurants.com
1270 Prospect Street   @EddieVsLJ
La Jolla, CA 92037
858.459.5500

- Inspired by the great classic seafood restaurants of New Orleans, San Francisco and Boston, Eddie V's offers the freshest seafood right off the docks, and USDA prime, center-cut steaks, aged 28 days and broiled to perfection.
- Operating with breathtaking views over the La Jolla Cove, executive chef Bill Greenwood focuses on local California ingredients and modern American culinary techniques infused into traditional dishes.
- Maine lobster tacos, jumbo lump crab cake, Georges Bank lemon sole, and the steaks are among the must try items.

Empire House

Comfort Food
127 University Avenue
San Diego, CA 92103
619.688.9283

www.empirehousesd.com
@EmpireHouseSD

- Serving up gourmet versions of comfort street food, owners Susie Baggs and Larry Malone (also the chef) offer customers the food they crave in a rustic, homelike environment.
- With a laser like focus on high quality food and exemplary customer service, Malone and Baggs sought to create a neighborhood hangout where customers would want to return day after day. Mission accomplished!
- Raved about items include the combo burger, the T.J. style hot dog, sausage bread, and the ahi tuna taco, voted one of the best in San Diego.

Flying Pig Pub & Kitchen

Gastropub
626 South Tremont Street
Oceanside, CA 92054
760.453.2940

www.flyingpigpubkitchen.com
@flyingpigpubkit

- Husband and wife owners, Roger and Aaron Browning, bring a slice of creativity to the Oceanside dining scene while offering rustic cuisine with a focus on local produce.
- The Flying Pig is a member of the Slow Food Movement; a global, grassroots movement with thousands of members around the world that links the pleasure of food with a commitment to community and the environment.
- Chef Mario Moser (Nine-Ten Restaurant and Bar) offers a hearty menu with staples like molasses braised pork belly, shrimp + grits, pork burger, and chicken and dumplings.

Searsucker

New American
611 5th Avenue
San Diego, CA 92101
619.233.7327

www.searsucker.com
@searsucker

- The new restaurant from Top Chef finalist, chef Brian Malarkey, Searsucker serves New American Classic cuisine, emphasizing approachable and unpretentious dishes paired with local craft beer, and a selection of one-of-a-kind wines from all over the world.
- The 7,000 square foot space is comfortable and warm – yet classic, using architectural salvage, distressed furniture and exposed ceiling beams to create an open warehouse feeling.
- Malarkey creates a menu of local fare, including seafood caught just minutes away on the San Diego coast. Items include the ribeye tomahawk, mahi mahi "baja", Alaskan halibut, and jalapeno-chorizo corn off the cob.

For a complete list of San Diego food resources, visit kundaeats.com/sandiego.

102

AQ

Seasonal American
1085 Mission Street
San Francisco, CA 94103
415.341.9000

www.aq-sf.com
@aqrestaurant_sf

- AQ stands for "as quoted," restaurant industry parlance for market price.
- "Seasonal" is the keyword for chef-owner Mark Liberman's (La Folie) latest project. Indeed, Northern California produce and meat availability dictates the protean menu, but AQ takes the concept even further by switching dishware and re-modeling the interior of the restaurant to match the season.
- Liberman favors Mediterranean and French technique, offering up dishes like guinea hen terrine and roasted rabbit with foie gras.

Boxing Room

Cajun-Creole
399 Grove Street
San Francisco, CA 94102
415.430.6590

www.boxingroom.com
@BoxingRoomSFSign

- Situated in the historical Standard Shirts Factory building, the Boxing Room is the latest project from The Absinthe Group.
- Channeling his Southern Louisiana heritage, chef Justin Simoneaux (The Moss Room) composes ingredient-driven Cajun and Creole dishes.
- Recommended dishes include smoked chicken andouille gumbo, shrimp po' boys, and fried chicken with black-eyed peas and collards.

Locanda

Roman Italian   www.locandasf.com
557 Valencia Street   @LocandaSF
San Francisco, CA 94110
415.863.6800

- Dubbed a "Roman inspired osteria and bar," owner Craig Stoll (Delfina) brings real Lazio cuisine to the Mission district.
- Chef Anthony Strong stays mostly true to the Roman tradition but modernizes dishes with novel ingredients and technique.
- The "Qvinto Qvarto" section of the menu provokes adventurous diners with offal choices like oxtails alla vaccinara, beef tripe with pecorino, and fried sweetbreads.
- Classic contorni sides (borlotti beans, grilled corn) perfectly complement the main meat dishes.

Locavore

New American   www.locavoreca.com
3215 Mission Street   @locavoreca
San Francisco, CA 94110
415.821.1918

- After fourteen years working in IT, Mario Duarte returns to his family's old restaurant (El Bramadero), completely overhauling the approach.
- True to its namesake, Locavore offers up sustainable, intensely seasonal food without breaking the bank. Chef Jonathan Merritt (Pok Pok) has quickly gained a reputation for his renditions of American classics like the humble cheeseburger (humanely raised beef, local white cheddar, house-cured bacon, caramelized onions, and aioli).

Nojo

Japanese   www.nojosf.com
231 Franklin Street   @nojosf
San Francisco, CA 94102
415.896.4587

- While traveling through Japan, chef-owner Greg Dunmore (Bacchanalia, Ame) developed the inspiration for Nojo.
- Nojo (Japanese for "farm") is a combination izakaya and yakitori grill, using local Bay Area ingredients. Grilled chicken (of all cuts) skewers are the house specialty.
- The wait service employs a unique teamwork approach, where the roles of the kitchen and front staff can be interchangeable.
- A diverse craft sake menu is smartly arranged.

Park Tavern

New American   www.parktavernsf.com
1652 Stockton Street   @parktavernsf
San Francisco, CA 94133
415.989.7300

- Overlooking North Beach's Washington Square, Park Tavern offers upscale American tavern food. This is the second successful restaurant partnership between Anna Weinberg and Jennifer Puccio (Marlowe).
- The small plates portion of the menu is organized by preparation method (smoked, raw, or fried). The bacon and chives deviled eggs have already achieved cult status.
- Chef Puccio maintains an open kitchen, showing off a wood-fired oven for roasting meats, seafood, and vegetables.
- The restaurant pays homage to the previous restaurant owner Ed Moose with a bar stool tribute.

Txoko

Spanish-Basque   www.txokosf.com
504 Broadway   @TXOKOsf
San Francisco, CA 94133
415.500.2744

- Txokos are Basque gastronomical societies where members gather to cook, experiment, eat, and socialize. It was the dream of co-owners Ryan Maxey and Ian Begg (Cafe Majestic, Naked Lunch) to channel the spirit of txokos through their new gastro bar.
- Interpretive Basque dishes are composed using premium California ingredients.
- While smaller pintxos plates (braised octopus, crispy pork headcheese, oysters) lay the foundation for the menu, a giant Txuleton bone in rib eye steak is available for the hungry.

For a complete list of San Francisco food resources, visit kundaeats.com/ sanfrancisco.

Raaga
Northern Indian   www.raagacuisine.com
544 Agua Fria Street
Santa Fe, NM 87501
505.820.6440

- Chef Pramod "Paddy" Rawal (also owner of Mumbai in East Lansing, MI) exemplifies the globetrotting chef, having worked in India, Egypt, London, Dubai, and Australia.
- While Rawal's main influence is northern Indian, he still manages to remember his surroundings and utilizes local Southwest elements.
- Raaga's menu has something for everyone and includes vegetarian and vegan options as well as meat and seafood choices.

For a complete list of Santa Fe food resources, visit kundaeats.com/santafe.

Altura

Italian   www.alturarestaurant.com
617 Broadway East
Seattle, WA 98102
206.402.6749

- Altura updates its menu weekly as chef Nathan Lockwood (Acquerello, Fork, The Ruins) interprets classic Italian dishes using seasonal Northwest proteins and vegetables.
- The menu employs the Italian methodology where diners choose from three, four, or five courses (plus amuse bouche) from a set list.
- Altura is the Italian word for "heights" as in "reaching for..."

Book Bindery

New American   www.bookbinderyrestaurant.com
198 Nickerson Street   www.almquistfamilyvintners.com
Seattle, WA 98109
206.283.2665

- From the outside, it looks like the opening credits to the Office (BBC), but inside this converted book bindery is a real beauty featuring an indoor greenhouse and water views of the Fremont Ship Canal.
- Native son Shaun McCrain (Taillevent, Per Se, Michael Mina) returns to Seattle, bringing with him an impressive modern cuisine resume. Dishes like duo of rabbit (loin and confit leg wrapped in bacon) and grilled Mishima Farms "flavor curve" wagyu are indulgent.
- The Book Bindery is the companion restaurant of the Almquist Family Vintners, so expect dishes that pair well with the winemaker's award winning Grenache.

Copperleaf Restaurant

New American   www.cedarbrooklodge.com
18525 36th Avenue South
Seattle, WA 98188
206.214.4282

- With a driven commitment to sustainable practices, Copperleaf Restaurant & Bar is a true Pacific Northwest farm-ranch-foraged woods-sea–to-table concept working directly with their network of independent suppliers.
- Executive Chef Mark Bodinet (French Laundry, Winnetu Inn and Resort) crafts the menu accentuating the strengths and availability of the Pacific bounty ingredients.
- Located near the Sea-Tac airport within the Cedarbrook Lodge, the property's ambiance is created by the large centerpiece stone fireplace and window views of locally made Boeing planes in the sky.

Hitchcock

New American   www.hitchcockrestaurant.com
133 Winslow Way East #100   @HitchcockResto
Bainbridge Island, WA 98110
206.201.3789

- Seattle foodies eagerly jump on the Bainbridge Island ferry to sample chef Brendan McGill's free-form tasting menus that are customized based on naming your price.
- Hitchcock celebrates island "localism" by sourcing ingredients from resident organic farms and fishing boats (the names of the suppliers proudly printed on the menu). Their motto: "We cook the food that surrounds us."
- The name of the restaurant honors the Hitchcock surname, one of the original founding families of the island.

Revel

Korean   www.revelseattle.com
403 North 36th Street   @revelseattle
Seattle, WA 98103
206.547.2040

- Husband and wife chefs, Seif Chirchi and Rachel Yang (Alain Ducasse at the Essex House, Joule), merge Korean and French flavors to create a truly contemporary American dining experience.
- Korean classics such as pajeon, bibimbap and mandoo are re-imagined with ingredients like cauliflower ricotta, fennel kimchi, and king oyster mushroom confit.
- With the majority of the dishes under $20, the location draws eager locals from the Fremont- Ballard neighborhoods.

Skillet Street Food and Diner

Diner   www.skilletstreetfood.com
1400 East Union Street   @skilletstfood
Seattle, WA 98122
206.512.2000

- Spawned from the pioneer food trailer, chef Josh Henderson finds a permanent home in Capitol Hill for his beloved Skillet Street Food.
- Food trailer classics remain on the menu such as waffles topped with fried egg and maple braised pork belly, but the physical brick-and-mortar location opens up interesting possibilities, including a full service bar.
- The signature Bacon Jam (pureed rendered bacon with spices and onion) has gained such cult status in Seattle that it is now available for retail and mail order.

The Walrus and the Carpenter

Oyster Bar   www.thewalrusbar.com
4743 Ballard Avenue Northwest   @thewalrusbar
Seattle, WA 98107
206.395.9227

- Fully leveraging geographic proximity, chef Renee Erickson (Boat Street) delivers a myriad of Northwestern oyster breeds on ice to the historic Ballard Avenue district.
- The Walrus and the Carpenter received a number of national accolades in 2011 including "Best New Restaurants in America" honors by several national publications. Erickson was also nominated for the James Beard Award (Best Chef, Northwest).
- Pickled vegetables are the sides of choice.

Where Ya At Matt

Creole Food Truck   www.whereyaatmatt.com
Seattle, WA   @whereyaatmatt
Variable Locations (check website)
No phone listed

- Who dat food truck? Where Ya At Matt specializes in mobile Creole dishes infused with New Southern technique.
- Chef Matthew Lewis (Highlands Bar and Grill, Hot and Hot Fish Club) draws upon recipes from his New Orleans childhood with classics such as etouffee, gumbo, jambalaya, and seafood po' boys.
- For dessert, the deep-fried Beignets sprinkled in powder sugar are mandatory.

For a complete list of Seattle food resources, visit kundaeats.com/seattle.

Ciro's Speakeasy and Supper Club
American Bar
2109 Bayshore Boulevard
Tampa, FL 33606
813.251.0022

- Ciro's Speakeasy, the latest collaboration between noted Tampa restaurateur Gordon Davis and partner Ro Patel, will make you feel as if you've gone back in time to the Prohibition era.
- Be prepared to give the valet the secret password in order to get through the plain wooden door.
- For the full experience, sit in one of the private, curtained off booths, adding to the secrecy and atmosphere.
- Dishes include duck leg confit, Greek-style calamari with octopus, and pork belly pizza.
- Priding itself on its secrecy, you won't find any website.

For a complete list of Tampa food resources, visit kundaeats.com/tampa.

112

Brady Tavern

Gastropub   www.taverntulsa.com
201 North Main Street   @BradyTavern
Tulsa, OK 74103
918.949.9801

- Located in the old Fox Hotel building, Chef Grant Vespasian's (Palace Café, Polo Grill) latest venture offers classic pub fare with a gourmet flavor.
- Using locally sourced, fresh ingredients, the seasonal menu offers signature dishes such as roast chicken, fish and frites, and the tavern burger, made using a proprietary grind of short rib and brisket.
- Mixologist Tony Collins offers pre prohibition era cocktails, artisan beers, or craft whiskeys from micro distilleries.

Juniper Restaurant & Martini Lounge

New American – Farm-to-Table   www.junipertulsa.com
324 East 3rd Street
Tulsa, OK 74120
918.794.1090

- Chef/Owner Justin Thompson (Sonoma Bistro & Wine Bar, The Brasserie) brings sophisticated dining to the downtown Tulsa area, offering fine food and martinis.
- Embracing a "Farm-to-Table" concept, Thompson sources the freshest, local ingredients available, while creating a menu that uses Italian, French, Spanish and American influences.
- As to be expected, the menu is seasonal and offers dishes such as sweet carrot soup, Oklahoma lamb, duck two ways, and bouillabaisse.
- The kitchen does run out of dishes at times, so be prepared.

Main Street Tavern

Gastropub   www.mainstreettavernba.com
200 South Main Street   @MainStTavernBA
Broken Arrow, OK 74012
918.872.1414

- Main Street Tavern is a collaboration between owners Jason and Kat Scarpa, and local chef Trevor Tack.
- Located in an early 20th century former drug store, Kat Scarpa used her skills as an architect to renovate the space by creating a custom bar, beautiful tin ceilings, and large windows that look out onto the town.
- The standard pub fare is available with items like burgers, meatloaf, and steaks, but it's the mac and cheese and the fish and chips that have received standout praise.

For a complete list of Tulsa food resources, visit kundaeats.com/tulsa.

America Eats

American
405 8th Street NW
Washington, DC 20004
202.393.0812

www.americaeatstavern.com
@americaeatstvrn

- In partnership with the National Archives' "What's Cooking, Uncle Sam?" exhibit, legendary chef José Andrés transforms the old Café Atlántico space into a pop-up celebration of the history of American cuisine.
- Dishes are developed using detailed historical recipes, for everything from the nation's founding (Colonial peanut soup) to modern times (buffalo wings). The menu features over eight different styles of catsup.
- This Penn Quarter restaurant will end its run on July 4, 2012.

Fiola

Italian
601 Pennsylvania Avenue NW
Washington, DC 20004
202.628.2888

www.fioladc.com
@fioladc

- The prodigal DC son returns. After stints in Manhattan (Fiamma, Four Seasons), Beard Foundation winning chef Fabio Trabocchi (Ritz Carlton's Maestro) opens his first owned restaurant in the heart of Penn Quarter.
- The "trattoria moderna" menu focuses on traditional Italian dishes using progressive technique and sourcing ideology. Trabocchi's calling cards are handmade pastas in foam and Le Marche-inspired seafood entrees.
- The deep fried ricotta and dough bomboloni with dolce dipping jars is a crowd favorite dessert.

Graffiato

Italian
707 6th Street NW
Washington, DC 20036
202.289.3600

www.graffiatodc.com
@graffiato

- Graffiato is Top Chef contestant Mike Isabella's tribute to his Italian nonna's cooking with a modern Jersey 2.0 twist.
- Menu highlights include pork charcuterie antipasti and fire kissed pizza (the speck topped Papa Smurf is smurfalicious). Chicken thighs with pepperoni sauce is television famous.
- Prosecco is delightfully served on tap.
- The two-story building in Chinatown features a giant first floor wood oven wraparound bar and a second floor cured ham station. Playful chef-patron interaction is encouraged.

Little Serow

Thai-Isaan
1511 17th Street NW
Washington, DC 20036

www.littleserow.com

- Greek food prodigy Johnny Monis delves into the spicy world of Issan style Northern Thai food.
- The fixed course (around seven), family style menu changes weekly and is posted online. Examples of dishes include jin tup (beef charred & hammered) and om gapi baan (shrimp in green curry). Pork ribs are the one constant.
- The small restaurant is located near Dupont Circle next to Monis' iconic Komi restaurant. Bargain basement (literally) prices and no-reservation policies draw crowds.

Pearl Dive Oyster Palace

Seafood-Oyster Bar   www.pearldivedc.com
1612 14th Street NW   @pearldivedc
Washington, DC 20009
202.319.1612

- Chef Jeff Black (Black Restaurant Group) brings this oyster speakeasy concept to 14th Street.
- The menu begins with a shucking huge variety of oyster species from across America (Beavertail, Cedar Island, Duckabush, Kumamoto, Kusshi, etc).
- Spicy Cajun seafood dishes round up the choices, but it's the stock and wine brined fried chicken that has created the foodie buzz.
- The Palace's charming vintage nautical decor has been carefully picked by antiquers and industrial recyclers.

Rogue 24

New American   www.rogue24.com
922 North Street NW   @rogue24dc
Washington, DC 20001
202.408.9724

- Rogue 24 was probably the most ambitious DC restaurant opening in 2011.
- Maverick chef RJ Cooper (The Oval Room, Vidalia) directs this 24 act culinary mini-series, complete with eclectic seasonal ingredients and couture preparations.
- Artisanal cocktail pairings for the two hour meal are courtesy of renowned mixologist Derek Brown.
- Tucked within Blagden Alley in the Shaw district, the location has an almost secret society feel.

Toki Underground

Japanese-Ramen   www.tokiunderground.com
1234 H Street NE 2nd Floor   @tokiunderground
Washington, DC 20002
202.388.3086

- Chef Erik Bruner-Yang's (Sticky Rice, Kushi) tiny second-floor H-Street ramen shop has become one of the hottest seats in the District.
- The hallmark bowl is the Toki hakata classic ramen featuring pork-loin chashu, vegetables, egg, and nori. The slurry Tonkotsu broth is slowly developed with pork bones, taking an entire day to develop.
- Graffiti-tagged walls, skateboard art, and a dj station give this space a panku rock feel.

Virtue Feed & Grain

Mediterranean   www.virtuefeedandgrain.com
106 South Union Street   @virtuefeed
Alexandria, VA 22314
571.970.3669

- Alexandria, Virginia restaurant magnates Meshelle and Cathal Armstrong (Restaurant Eve, Eamonn's Dublin Chipper, and the Majestic) open their fourth restaurant in Old Town.
- The "modern pub grub" menu has Irish and nose-to-tail influences with dishes like smoked haddock chowder, shagger's pie, and pig's feet.
- The name of the restaurant "Virtue" comes from the owners' aspirations to create tastes with "no evil" for surely "goodness and mercy" will follow.

For a complete list of Washington, DC food resources, visit kundaeats.com/dc.

Restaurants Alphabetically

(Restaurant, Page Number)

Restaurants by City

Restaurants by Food Category

(Restaurant, Page Number)

Verdea Restaurant & Wine
Bar 36

Asian
ChoLon Modern Asian Bistro
30
Hawkers Asian Street Fare 79
Pubbelly 56

Bakery
Sun Street Breads 61

BBQ
Bogart's Smokehouse 94
Heirloom Market BBQ 1
Jacque's Whistle Stop Cafe 43
Midwood Smokehouse 16

Belgian
Blue Monk 11
Cannibal 69
Leopold 21

Brazilian
Beta by Sabor 58

British
Owen & Engine 23
The Rumpus Room 58

Cajun-Creole
Boxing Room 103
Riverbend Restaurant & Bar
95
Tibby's New Orleans Kitchen
79
Where Ya At Matt 111

Cambodian
Sekong By Night 84

Canadian
M. Wells (closed) 73

Chinese
Mala Sichuan 39
Peter Chang's China Grill 17
RedFarm 73

Cuban
Gregoria's Kitchen and Cuban
Steakhouse 90

Ethiopian
Gosh Ethiopian Restaurant 43

French
Ai Fiori 68
Brasserie 19 38
Comme Ça 44
Dominique's on Magazine 65
The Indigo Duck 41
Jean-Robert's Table 25
La Promenade des Anglais 72
Little Bird 88
Maude's Liquor Bar 22
Menton 10
Petite Jacqueline 87
St. Jack 89

Gastropub
Beer Kitchen No. 1 42
Brady Tavern 113
Citizen Public House 83
Deagan's Kitchen & Bar 26
Flying Pig Pub & Kitchen 101
Main Street Tavern 114
The Monterey 99
Ollie Irene 7
Park Tavern 106

Acknowledgements

Special thanks to Brian Bassett and Jane Pratt for ace copy editing suggestions. Thanks to Robey Martin, Matt Sadler, and Don Carter for "book research" and a handsome bag. We'll always have Fredericksburg.